The Authentic Garden

The Authentic Garden

FIVE PRINCIPLES
FOR CULTIVATING A
SENSE OF PLACE

Claire E. Sawyers

Timber Press

Published in 2007 by

Timber Press, Inc.
The Haseltine Building
133 S.W. Second Avenue, Suite 450
Portland, Oregon 97204-3527, U.S.A.

www.timberpress.com

For contact information regarding editorial, marketing, sales, and distribution in the United Kingdom, see
www.timberpress.co.uk.

The author is grateful to the following publishers and copyright holders for
permission to use the selections reprinted in this book:

"Principles for my garden" from *Adventures of a Gardener* by Peter Smithers,
published by Harvill. Reprinted by permission of The Random House Group Ltd.

Extracts from *Where the Sky Began: Land of the Tallgrass Prairie* by John Madson, published by Sierra Club Books.
Reprinted by permission of Dycie J. Madson.

Printed in China

Library of Congress Cataloging-in-Publication Data

Sawyers, Claire.
  The authentic garden : five principles for cultivating a sense of place / Claire E. Sawyers.
      p. cm.
  Includes bibliographical references and index.
  ISBN-13: 978-0-88192-831-0
  1. Gardens--Design. I. Title.
  SB473.S29 2007
  712´.6--dc22   2007002628

A catalog record for this book is also available from the British Library.

Dedicated to Harrison Flint, Jules Janick, Fred Roberts, Richard Lighty, Saburo Sone, Jelena deBelder, Princess G. Sturdza, Prince Peter and Isabelle Wolkonsky, and Pamela Copeland—who all, firsthand, shaped my sensibilities and career path as a gardener and garden writer. And to my parents and grandparents, who taught me how to plant seeds.

CONTENTS

ACKNOWLEDGMENTS

I wish to acknowledge and express my gratitude to those gardeners championed in this book, who have captured the American spirit in their gardens and shared that spirit so generously with others. Rather than list them here, I will let you read on to discover their names and their gardens.

Any number of editors have helped develop my interest and joy in writing and photography over the course of my career. My thanks to them for their patience and encouragement. My thanks as well to the family members who kindly read and commented on each chapter despite long gaps between installments: my aunt, Janet Sawyers, and my mother, Betty Jane Sawyers.

Without the initial interest and encouragement from the staff at Timber Press, this project would not have commenced. I'd especially like to acknowledge the pleasure I've had working with Timber's editor-in-chief, Tom Fischer, and with the copyeditor, Lorraine Anderson, who certainly smoothed out what I gave her to work with while being very encouraging. My thanks for the opportunity to share these thoughts and observations with fellow garden creators.

INTRODUCTION

COMPARED TO COUNTRIES noted for their gardeners and gardens, the United States hasn't been at the art of garden making very long. So it's perhaps understandable that we come up short when we try to identify the essence of the American garden. The American gardening culture is still evolving; we're still defining the American gardening ethic and aesthetic. (Here, and throughout the book, when using the term *American* I'm referring primarily to one country of the Americas—the United States. While much of what I describe applies to other countries in the Americas, the examples used in this book come almost exclusively from the United States. In no way do I intend to slight the other cultures and countries of the Americas by restricting my use of this term; in fact, one of the finest public gardens created in recent years that honors and celebrates the cultural and natural heritage of its region is the Oaxaca Botanical Garden in Oaxaca, Mexico, but sadly, I don't have the knowledge to draw many such examples from American countries outside the United States.)

Think about French, Italian, English, Chinese, or Japanese gardens, and certain images, architectural characteristics, and garden objects quickly come to mind. The art of the pleasure garden in China was already well developed by the reign of Emperor Hsuan Wu (AD 500–515), when Ju Hao was described as a subtle craftsman who chose fine rocks, transplanted bamboo, and laid out trees to create gardens "to give the impression of rustic wilderness" (Kuck 1968, 60). The seminal Japanese work known as *Sakuteiki* or *Treatise of Garden Making* is believed to have been written in the mid-to-late eleventh century. In Europe, Islamic or Persian gardens were being built in Cordoba, Spain, by 756, when Abd-ar-Rahman I became the emir of Andalusia and set about making a garden based on his grandfather's garden in Damascus. By the eleventh century, work had commenced on the Alhambra in Granada. Even "younger" cultures in Europe have been making gardens for centuries. In Italy, the Botanical Garden of Padua, extant today, was created in 1545, and in France, Louis XIV commissioned André Le Nôtre in 1662 to design a garden for Versailles to surpass any garden known to humankind.

I've heard gardening described as "the slowest of the performing arts." When it takes decades for a single garden to mature, it follows that centuries are needed to develop a garden culture or aesthetic with the sophistication associated with the great gardening cultures of the world. European immigrants who founded the United States brought their cultures, including their concepts of shaping the land and gardens, with them. Not only did they name their new towns and villages after those they had left behind, they also began developing their houses and gardens based primarily on what they had known before. In 1741 Henry Middleton laid out what is said to be the oldest landscaped garden in America—Middleton Place, near today's Charleston, South Carolina. Around what remains of the plantation house today, symmetrical "butterfly lakes" made by herculean earth-moving efforts are still a marvel and something André Le Nôtre would have approved of. In the late 1700s, George Washington developed the grounds and gardens of Mount Vernon over a period of forty-five years, and Thomas Jefferson devoted more than forty years to developing Monticello. Both became celebrated models for Americans to emulate in developing home grounds. Both borrowed heavily from English Renaissance formal garden design, combined with the romantic and picturesque landscape ideals promulgated by Humphry Repton in England. Pleasure gardens in the new nation had little to do with a New World aesthetic and a lot to do with the Old World.

Referred to as "a mini-Versailles on the Brandywine," the garden developed by Alfred I. du Pont at Nemours in Wilmington, Delaware, between 1910 and 1930 borrowed heavily from French garden designs.

The house and gardens of Old Westbury in New York were inspired by English design.

The Italian Renaissance–style villa and garden known as Vizcaya, built by James Deering between 1912 and 1916, is grand evidence that the "cult of the Italian garden" had spread to America at the turn of the century.

The gardens of Filoli in Woodside, California, were inspired by Italian Renaissance design.

This pattern of borrowing persisted. A century later, affluent Americans traveled abroad and returned with ideas and inspiration. Pierre du Pont, founder of the Dupont Company and a descendant of French immigrants, created Longwood Gardens in Kennett Square, Pennsylvania, on a piece of ground he purchased in 1906. After travels to Europe, where he visited at least twenty Italian villas and fifty French chateaux, he developed an open-air theater by 1914 inspired by the outdoor theater at the Villa Gori in Italy, followed by elaborate Italian water gardens modeled on those he saw at Villa Gamberaia near Florence. Nearby, Alfred I. du Pont built a mansion by 1910 followed by gardens developed until the early 1930s and planned in part by his son, Alfred Victor, who studied garden design in Paris. With massive fountains, abundant statuary, temples, and a colonnade, it has been described as "a mini-Versailles on the Brandywine." This wasn't just happening near Philadelphia; in all parts of the United States, English and European influence held sway. In New York, John S. Phipps built a mansion in 1906 designed by British architect George Crawley and added impressive English-style gardens known today as Old Westbury Gardens. In the late 1800s, George Vanderbilt made his grand home, the Biltmore Estate outside Asheville, North Carolina, emulate the chateaux in France with parterres modeled on those of Vaux-le-Vicomte. In Miami, Florida, industrialist James Deering hired a thousand workers to build his Italian Renaissance–style villa, Vizcaya, between 1912 and 1916. The gardens contain an imported sixteenth-century Italian baroque fountain, Roman altars, and statues of mythological gods and goddesses from Italy. Even on the West Coast, wealthy San Franciscans Mr. and Mrs. William Bourn II built their home, known as Filoli, with sixteen acres of formal gardens, including an Italian Renaissance teahouse and walled gardens defined by hedges, columnar evergreens, and expansive lawns. Much as the founding fathers did a century before, these industrial leaders turned to English and European traditions for ideas on developing their own homes and gardens here. Since all these grand country estates today are public gardens, I could argue that they're still shaping and defining Americans' concepts of the ideal garden.

Edith Wharton wrote in *Italian Villas and Their Gardens*, published in 1904, about this wave of influence:

> The cult of the Italian garden has spread from England to America, and there is a general feeling that, by placing a marble bench here and a sun-dial there, Italian "effects" may be achieved. The results produced, even where much money and thought have been expended, are not altogether satisfactory; and some critics have thence inferred that the Italian garden is, so to speak, *untranslatable*, that it cannot be adequately rendered in another landscape and another age.
>
> Certain effects, those which depend on architectural grandeur as well as those due to coloring and age, are no doubt unattainable; but there is, nonetheless, much to be learned from the old Italian gardens, and the first lesson is that, if they are to be a real inspiration, they must be copied, not in the letter but in the spirit. That is, a marble sarcophagus and a dozen twisted columns will not make an Italian garden, but a piece of ground laid out and planted on the principles of the old garden craft will be, not indeed an Italian garden in the literal sense, but what is far better, *a garden as well adapted to its surroundings as were the models which inspired it*.
>
> This is the secret to be learned from the villas of Italy; and no one who has looked at them with this object in view will be content to relapse into vague admiration of their loveliness. (283)

Alter a few words in the preceding couple of paragraphs—that is, change them to say, for example, "The cult of the Japanese garden has spread . . . to America, and there is a general feeling that by placing a granite stone lantern here and a washbasin there, Japanese 'effects' may be achieved"—and the same could have been said about any number of garden styles in America at the start of the twentieth century or now at the start of the twenty-first. We are still heavily borrowing garden design inspiration. Look in the gardening section of any big bookstore and you will inevitably find numerous books on English, Irish, Italian, French, and Japanese gardens. Visit modern American public gardens, those created from scratch instead of converted from turn-of-the-century estates, and they too reflect this. At the Chicago Botanic Garden, built during the last several decades, six "rooms" in the English Walled Garden demonstrate styles of English gardens, and the heart of the property is Sansho-En, or "the garden of three islands," their famous Japanese garden. At the Dallas Arboretum and Botanical Garden, the 2.2-acre Mimi's Garden, "inspired by Gertrude Jekyll," opened in 1988 as a "Texas-style English cottage garden including perennials, native plants, roses, water features, etc.," as described in a job announcement for a gardener that year. (A two-acre cottage garden seems like an oxymoron, but because "Texas" is synonymous with "big," perhaps the Texan concept of space and scale has been incorporated into this application.)

A defining characteristic of American gardens, true through time, is simply that we copy from other cultures. Countless examples prove that we've done that very well, but we can do better. So this book is about how to make a garden, as Wharton wrote, "as well adapted to its surroundings as were the models which inspired it"—that is, how to learn from the great gardens of the world and extract their lessons rather than mimic their look. More than that, this book is a plea to do so. This is about how to make gardens true to a place, a time, and a culture—that is, to capture and reflect a certain authentic spirit, so that in turn these gardens will nurture the spirits of those who frequent them.

Wharton's frustration came from seeing Italian gardens superficially copied; mine comes most personally from seeing Japanese gardens copied. I lived in Japan for six years and for a period worked with a Japanese landscaping firm in Kyoto. Once I returned to the United States, homeowners wanted my advice on making a Japanese garden, but I had little interest in contributing to the creation of geographical confusion. (A friend of mine at the time said, "Tell them to move to Japan; that's how they can have a Japanese garden.") I began to realize that it's not obvious how to extract the profound lessons of great gardens and then sensibly apply them. It is all too easy to focus on the artifacts of a garden and miss the underlying characteristics and principles that make us—the visitors—long for our own surroundings to have some of the same qualities. We come away simply concluding that we want an Italian garden or a Japanese garden without asking ourselves why we feel that way.

This is not to say that we shouldn't look to great gardens and great gardeners for inspiration. Managers and leaders who want to have proficient companies read about, visit, and study other successful companies to see what they can learn, but learning from a Fortune 500 company making widgets doesn't mean you return to your own company and start manufacturing widgets. Rather, you adapt and apply to your own situation what you've learned about the process or the management systems. We travel for pleasure, seeking experiences in other cultures and exploring their artistic expressions. Inevitably we're influenced and shaped by those experiences and inspired by those expressions, as our garden history reveals. But the history of American garden making has largely resulted from those who have visited great foreign gardens coming home and doing the equivalent of making widgets. This book, I hope, will help you start making a garden uniquely suited to the landscape of your region.

I'm indebted to the late Sir Peter Smithers, although I never met him, for outlining his clear principles to garden by and for setting an example that has inspired me. A career politician, he developed a celebrated garden at Vico Morcote in Switzerland and wrote with indelible clarity about how he did it. In an article I clipped out of a magazine years ago, he outlined the ten personal "commandments" he held dear and followed in creating his own garden. He reiterated them in his book, *Adventures of a Gardener* (1995, 2–3):

1. The garden shall be a source of pleasure to the owner and his friends, not a burden and an anxiety.

2. It must therefore be planted so as to reduce labor to an absolute minimum, and the amount of work must diminish as the owner grows older.

3. Any plants like palms or conifers that would contradict the nature of the surrounding deciduous forest should be rigidly excluded.

4. All plants in the garden must be of a permanent kind: no annuals, biennials, or plants requiring lifting in winter or special attention.

5. The planting must be dense so that the plants live in a self-sustaining community with one another, with little space for weeds to grow and little need for support.

6. The plantings will be varying compositions according to the lie of the land with no repetition. The visitor should be surprised at every turn of the path with a new plant community different from what he has seen so far.

7. At all levels planting distances are such as to form a canopy.

8. No plant is added to the garden if there is in existence an obtainable superior form.

9. Difficult plants, if not successful after a fair trial, should be abandoned for easier subjects of which there are plenty.

10. No plant is ever sold or exchanged. All plants are available to serious gardeners, stock and labor permitting. The pleasure of owning a fine plant is not complete until it has been given to friends.

Smithers's principles deal with practical aspects of what I would call the collector's or plantsman's garden. I offer in the following chapters only half as many principles as Sir Peter Smithers, but I hope they share some measure of his clarity and his purpose of helping fellow gardeners. The five principles I set forth, each treated in a separate chapter, are as follows:

1. Capture the sense of place.

2. Derive beauty from function.

3. Use humble or indigenous materials.

4. Marry the inside to the outside.

5. Involve the visitor.

The final chapter showcases gardens where these principles have been applied, creating distinctly American gardens.

This book won't tell you how deep your perennial border should be or when to prune clematis. Numerous books are available that give practical advice on the growing of plants. Instead, this book offers practical advice and inspiration on creating a garden that truly belongs to you, the gardener, to your home, and to the region in which you (and the garden) live. In offering this advice, I assume you're interested in creating a surrounding that feeds your soul, and that you derive or want to derive gratification and a deep sense of satisfaction from your environment. If you think of your garden as a meaningful individualistic expression that carries with it some responsibilities for stewardship, the ideas presented here may be helpful.

These thoughts and suggestions have grown out of my exposure to the public horticulture profession and a series of fortunate work experiences. After enrolling at Purdue University as a horticulture major, I took a semester off to return to Japan, where I had lived for six years in Tokyo as a youngster with my family, to work with a Japanese landscaper. I thereby combined my interest in horticulture with my familiarity with a great gardening culture. I was fortunate enough to work in the Sone-Zoen, or Sone landscaping company, reporting to Saburo Sone, one of three brothers in business together in the Kyoto-Osaka area who designed and installed residential and commercial landscapes and also took care of the famous Zen garden at Tenryu-ji (Temple of the Heavenly Dragon) on the outskirts of Kyoto. When I returned from that experience, I realized I didn't want to encourage the idea of American gardeners copying verbatim the look of Japanese gardens; instead I wanted to help gardeners translate to the American landscape what it was about those gardens that made us want to emulate them. Once I graduated from college, I spent a year working in gardens in Belgium and France and visiting many of the classic and historic gardens of Europe. Again, the challenge was to identify what the "take home" messages were, or what could be successfully borrowed and applied in my homeland. This book draws from those and two subsequent opportunities: work at the Mount Cuba Center near Greenville, Delaware, a naturalistic garden emphasizing plants native to the Piedmont region of the United States that was developed as the private residence of Mr. and Mrs. Lammot du Pont Copeland but is now open to the public; and the Scott Arboretum, the campus of Swarthmore College, in Swarthmore, Pennsylvania, a type of landscape almost uniquely developed in the United States.

Capture the Sense of Place

TO GARDEN with a sense of place means to discover and preserve what is special about your site, its *genius loci*. This means working with what you've been given, not struggling against it. In most instances, honoring a sense of place means learning about the natural and cultural history of your area.

DISCOVERING THE *GENIUS LOCI*

Genius loci is Latin for "the peculiar character of a place with reference to the impression that it makes on the mind: the spirit that rests in a place; guardian of the place," according to the *Random House College Dictionary*. To capture and celebrate the sense of place, or *genius loci*, you have to become an observer and come to a site with no preconceived ideas about what the design of your house or garden will be. You'll determine the design by a process of discovery and by observing the special characteristics of the site, then allowing those to shape the most appropriate way to develop the house and garden there. The design will be a response to what you find and appreciate there, not an imposition from outside.

This approach has been advocated and modeled by a number of notable American designers over the last few decades. In the late 1920s, long before the environmental movement became identifiable as such, Edith Roberts, who was a professor of botany at Vassar College, and Elsa Rehmann, who was a landscape architect, tried to teach homeowners a sensitivity to site in a series of twelve articles they wrote for *House Beautiful*. These articles were compiled and published in 1929 as a small book titled *American Plants for American Gardens*. Their pertinent lessons have been made accessible again with a 1996 reprinting of the book. Eleven of the twelve chapters each look at one type of landscape or natural habitat, identifying its defining characteristics. Each of these chapters then outlines the kinds of plants found in that particular habitat, distills the visual characteristics of the site, and translates these into harmonious architectural characteristics and complementary building materials. If you accept that your house is your most important garden feature, you will realize that it too must capture a sense of place. Roberts and Rehmann show how to go about designing a house that captures the sense of place in several of the distinct habitats they outline.

For example, they suggest that an open field

> needs . . . a country house that is in spirit with it. Such a house should have the architectural simplicity of a farmstead especially of the early American type. Sometimes the house can be really an old one. Sometimes it is freshly designed in the old manner with low and broad stretched lines, with roofs and gables that fit the rolling topography and with wide terraces. Often a great old tree shelters it and throws its shadows across it. Out beyond in the sunshine the fields can then be one luxurious mass of flowers. (18–19)

Regarding the juniper hillside type of landscape, which would include poor farm fields no longer under cultivation with the dominant plant being eastern red cedar (*Juniperus virginiana*), they point out that

> such a hillside is full of possibilities when it becomes the site for a house. It can influence the style and can control the shape of the rooflines, the plan and the materials. In this way, the building becomes one with its surroundings. Under the sway of the rugged picturesqueness, the house becomes low, and wide-spread so that it nestles into the hillside. . . . Dark brown shingles can blend with the green of cedars, stucco can take its tone from the color of the ledges, stone can be hewn from the rocks themselves. (27–28)

In white pine forests and plantations, they suggest using needle-covered paths and creeping ground covers with "views that are framed by tall trees." What kind of buildings fit in such a scene? Log cabins and lodges: "They can be inconspicuous, almost invisible even at a short distance, among the rocks and in the shadowy depth of the woods" (41).

By contrast, homes in oak woodlands should be harmonized with the landscape using "weathered shingles, blackish slate, dark oak, soft-toned stucco, handmade brick or stone" (47). Further, "ells and wings" should mimic the rolling contours of land.

In the open fields of upstate New York, Jack Potter and David Leib wanted their house to fit in with the character of the surrounding farmsteads. The house's design borrows from the vernacular barns in the region to help it fit in.

A modern log cabin tucked in the woods has a personality that fits harmoniously with its surroundings, being "inconspicuous . . . and in the shadowy depth of the woods," as advocated by Edith Roberts and Elsa Rehmann in *American Plants for American Gardens*.

These examples and the other landscapes that Roberts and Rehmann describe—including gray birch thickets, beech-maple-hemlock woods, and hemlock ravines—are characteristic of the eastern United States. While the various chapters of the book don't necessarily apply to other parts of the country, they do help illustrate how to become sensitive to the *genius loci* and responsive to the site.

While these two women's strong writings remain, their design work has been lost or remains obscure. By contrast, innumerable examples of the work of one of America's most notable architects, one whose designs manifest the concepts conveyed in the writings of Roberts and Rehmann, survive today. Frank Lloyd Wright created buildings in harmony with their surroundings; he responded to and captured the *genius loci* so successfully in his designs that his work includes some of America's most cherished and celebrated houses. His approach speaks even more strongly today to our emotional need and desire to reconnect to nature than when he originally designed and built such properties, I believe. This kind of sensitivity explains his lasting and posthumously growing popularity. To visit Taliesin West, his home and studio outside of Scottsdale, Arizona, is to learn how he adjusted building techniques used in his midwestern experiences to the climate and soils of the desert. "If you are building in the desert, the best foundation is right *on* the desert. Don't dig into it and break it," he wrote in *The Natural House* (1954, 142). Details of the desert flora also shaped the aesthetics of his buildings in Arizona: the saguaro cactus ridges and spines, in part, inspired the ridges and lines of his buildings there. On the other hand, the expansiveness of the prairies is expressed in the low-slung hip-roofed "prairie ranches" he designed for sites in Illinois. Then there's Fallingwater, outside Pittsburgh, Pennsylvania, a masterpiece of designing in response to the site. Imagine building a replica of Fallingwater someplace else and you quickly realize that its design is so dependent on the site, so site specific, little could be transported and recreated elsewhere. Fallingwater is the antithesis of the cookie-cutter houses we see in subdivision developments from coast to coast.

There are scores of new books on Frank Lloyd Wright and his designs, but let us listen to his own words from *The Natural House* as he describes the need for this kind of sensitivity in design, which he calls "integrity in architecture." (Note that Wright's term *Usonian* comes from the acronym USONA for United States of North America. His Usonian houses were designed for the middle class and relied on basic, readily available materials such as concrete, glass, plywood, and brick.)

> The Usonian house, then, aims to be a natural performance, one that is integral to site; integral to environment; integral to the life of the inhabitants. A house integral with the nature of materials—wherein glass is used as glass, stone as stone, wood as wood—and all the elements of the environment go into and throughout the house. (134)

Another notable designer who developed an ethic or design approach responsive to the site, much like Frank Lloyd Wright did with his buildings, is Jens

The style of roof on this Salt Lake City, Utah, house reflects the character of the inspiring mountains beyond. In both its pitch and the pattern of its shingles, the roof speaks to the *genius loci*.

Taliesin West, near Scottsdale, Arizona. Frank Lloyd Wright believed that a building should harmonize with its surroundings, respond to its site, and be integral with its environment to have integrity. In designing with those beliefs, he gave us this example in the West as well as examples in the East and the Midwest that capture and manifest a sense of place.

Fallingwater, near Pittsburgh, Pennsylvania.

Jensen, a contemporary of Wright's. Described as the dean of American landscape architecture and considered by many to be America's most important landscape architect, Jensen immigrated to the United States from Denmark in 1884 at the age of twenty-four. During the period when Frank Lloyd Wright had a studio in Oak Park, Illinois, Jensen became the chief landscape architect for the Chicago

Taliesin East, Spring Green, Wisconsin.

Park District; and like Wright, Jensen was a proponent of drawing inspiration from the site and building harmoniously with nature and the ecological processes of the site. His gem of a book, *Siftings*, originally published in 1939, like *American Plants for American Gardens* has become a classic and has been reprinted. In it he expresses this principle:

> Local color, the expression of the environments dear to us and of which we are a part, must be reflected in creative landscaping and be its motive. Through generations of evolution our native landscape becomes a part of us and out of this we may form fitting compositions for our people. (6)

With this philosophy and approach, one might assume that as a landscape architect Jensen set about recreating or restoring natural areas, but he was equally clear that this approach doesn't mean trying to duplicate nature:

> Nature is not to be copied—man cannot copy God's out-of-doors. He can interpret its message in a composition of living tones. The real worth of a landscaper lies in his ability to give to humanity the blessing of nature's spiritual values, as they are interpreted in his art. The field

The pattern and variation of rocks at the edge of a stream or river may provide inspiration for creating a garden stream.

is boundless, and there is no need of importing from foreign shores. To the true artist it is a great adventure into the mysteries of an unknown world. (15)

Jensen reshaped many of the large Chicago parks between 1906 and 1918 to express the essence or capture the sense of the American heartland through interpretation and artistic expression rather than mimicry. After his retirement in 1935 at the age of seventy-five, Jensen established The Clearing in Ellison Bay, Wisconsin, a "folk school" where he wanted people to be able to come and learn in a natural setting. Jensen designed its lodge and schoolhouse in collaboration with renowned architect Hugh Garden, and all buildings are of log or native stone, blending with the rustic natural setting. Jensen thought that in this place individuals could develop sound values for their lives and professions, because he believed that environments have a profound impact on people and that understanding one's own ecology and culture leads to clear thinking. He and Wright were part of a group of designers, architects, and landscape architects who were collectively referred to as the Prairie School, a movement based on regionally oriented designs.

Rocks dripping with water, such as these along the Blue Ridge Parkway in North Carolina, may provide a model in nature to abstract from to create a water feature such as the one at Ashland Hollow, a private garden in Delaware.

The year Jensen died, 1951, another landscape architect whose work helps demonstrate this principle, A. E. Bye, opened his office. His practice and work have been documented in his book, *Art into Landscape, Landscape into Art*, published in 1983. Besides documenting his projects, Bye's book contains a series of photographs of landscapes expressing to him a variety of moods, further illustrating how he observed landscapes and interpreted their character—how he learned to "listen" to the landscape. Images of trees and forests depict "elegance," leaves and bare branches show "brittleness," bogs and solitary boulders say "mystery," and bright meadows mean "dazzle."

Ian McHarg, probably more than any other designer, spent his life trying to teach the importance of designing in harmony with nature. His 1969 book, *Design with Nature,* presented a way for professional land planners, landscape architects, and builders to design based on an understanding of place, and it articulated the profound ecological need to do so. In time, his planning approach came to be known as the McHarg Method and helped shape forty years of students in the University of Pennsylvania's Department of Landscape Architecture. There he taught students to identify the physical and biological processes that shape a place and that should be regarded as instrumental in determining site-sensitive design. He advocated collecting and interpreting basic data on climate, geology, physical features, hydrology, soils, plant ecology, wildlife habitats, historical monuments, and land use in a value system to determine design pros and cons.

As these master designers have shown us, capturing the sense of place in a building (or city) plan or landscape layout requires having and knowing a specific site. If you don't already have a site, you may have a list of goals or desires to help you select a site. For instance, if you want to have a meadow garden, you'll want to seek out a site with some open sunny areas. Cookie-cutter house plans are dropped onto sites in many regions of the country regardless of the area's unique characteristics, but this is doing things in reverse and is likely to result in mismatches and ultimately less-than-gratifying results when it comes to drawing nourishment for the soul from your property or living in harmony with nature.

WHY THIS IS HARDER THAN IT SOUNDS

With the experience of these masters who have laid the groundwork since at least the 1920s to draw on, why do we still see so much development detached from site? I believe it has something to do with the fact that the birth of today's American pleasure garden was predicated on the conquering, taming, and containing of nature. As European settlers moved to this country, they harvested and cleared the dense eastern deciduous woods to create pastures and fields, and they distanced the threats of wilderness for the sake of survival.

William Cronon, in *Changes in the Land: Indians, Colonists, and the Ecology of New England* (1983), describes methods early settlers employed to rid the landscape of mature forest. The simplest approach was to girdle the trees. This would kill the trees, allowing corn to be planted between the trunks, and in subsequent years as time and energy allowed, the trunks could be felled. By the late 1700s, settlers were cutting the trees down using axes and then burning the land to remove the brush and undergrowth. Ultimately they sawed up and removed the trunks or burned them further.

Given the importance of creating field and pasture for the production of food, and the time and effort required to do so, preventing regeneration—nature's re-claiming of fields—must have been strongly ingrained and taught to subsequent generations. Thus, the physical effort expended to change forest to field must have shaped basic attitudes toward wilderness. The forests of the eastern United States also had a powerful psychological effect on the first European settlers, although this is hard to relate to today when so little remains and we're so removed from wilderness in our daily lives. John Madson, in *Where the Sky Began: Land of the Tallgrass Prairie* (1982), reminds us that one of the first things that the new colonists must have known, as anchor chains rumbled down through hawseholes, was that they had never really seen trees before. Wherever they had begun—in the snug shires of England, the meadows of Brittany, or the diked fields of Holland—they had seen nothing to compare with this wall of forest that rose behind the coast of America. . . . a limitless wilderness of trees, the infinite and forbidding sweep of forest that extended from the portals of the New World as far west as any man knew, and beyond, the greatest forest that western man had seen during the Christian era. . . .

The infinity of trees reached from the Spanish Sea to the barrens of Hudson Bay, and westward into lands scarcely imagined, with some trees towering nearly 200 feet above open forest floors that were too shaded for undergrowth. Many years later Francis Parkman would call it "vast, continuous, dim and silent as a cavern." It was said that a gray squirrel could travel inland from the Atlantic coast for nearly a thousand miles and never touch the ground. Old novels tell of the "pale woodsmen" of the eastern forests—not a reflection of race, but of lives spent under the trees. (3–4)

Madson's recounting of the impressions of settlers who reached the prairie reveals what a strikingly different effect open prairie had on the mind:

The gaiety of the prairie, its embellishments and the absence of gloom and savage wildness of the forest, all contribute to dispel the feeling of loneliness which usually creeps over the mind of the solitary traveler in the wilderness. Though he may not see a house or a human being, and is conscious that he is far from the habitation of man, the traveler upon the prairie can scarcely divest himself of the idea that he is traveling through scenes embellished by the hand of art. (15)

Wrestling with nature and shaping it into submission helped define American heroes—think about the story of Paul Bunyan or the builders of the Hoover Dam. After three hundred years of taming and conquering nature, sadly, that way of relating to nature has become part of the American psyche. Wilderness is a part of the American spirit; it and our relationship to it defines in large part who we are.

Look at the typical American suburban home and contemplate the amount of mowing, clipping, and containing required to maintain it, and you'll understand that the legacy of controlling and conquering nature is still evident in our backyards, even if true wilderness seems far removed. While modern Americans are still controlling nature or attempting to, we've also finally realized, perhaps too late in many instances, that nature no longer needs to be eliminated to carve out a safe and comfortable place to live. Now it needs to be protected and cherished if it and we are going to survive. We know natural and wilderness areas need to be nurtured not only for the foods and the resources they provide, but for their contribution to meeting our spiritual needs as well. For our mental well-being, we need wilderness and natural areas to feel our place, to soothe our souls, and to give us a glimpse of what has defined us.

In his 1949 classic, *A Sand County Almanac*, Aldo Leopold described wilderness as "the raw material out of which man has hammered the artifact called civilization" (188). So without a sense or remnant of wilderness, how do we preserve an understanding and appreciation of where we've come from? Leopold's plea was for "the preservation of some tag-ends of wilderness, as museum pieces, for the edification of those who may one day wish to see, feel, or study the origins of their cultural inheritance" (188).

Modern American gardens that provide a sense of wilderness and the feeling that while mother nature has been "on the run" (as Neil Young sang in his 1970 tune "After the Gold Rush"), it hasn't yet completely vanished, can be deeply reassuring. A backyard Eden helps restore our connection to nature. While our struggles to preserve open land and wilderness in national parks express the realization that nature should no longer be conquered and pushed back, that shift hasn't yet happened in most backyard gardens across America and certainly not in our front yards. My plea is for us to realize that we can preserve a sense of cultural inheritance not just in our national parks but also in our backyards.

DEVELOPING THE SKILL AND SENSITIVITY

To become sensitive to the character of a site and then "interpret it in your art," as Jens Jensen would have it, first get to know your site; become intimate with it. Perhaps all the dimensions considered in the McHarg Method represent more information than you need for a single house or home garden, but going through the exercise of inventorying the site in as many ways as you can will change your awareness and perceptions of it and perhaps shape your response to it in some unpredictable ways. For instance: what is the track of the sun in summer and winter and how will it illuminate the house and garden areas? Where are the shade lines? Where are the wet sites and rocky sites? Where are the opportunities for borrowed views? Does wind affect the site? If so, how? Only by first knowing your garden site can you make decisions that will capture and celebrate the sense of the place versus imposing a design unrelated and unresponsive to the site.

Here are some inexpensive ways to understand your site on your own:

~ Make a map or a drawing of your property noting all the existing plants, then make one of other natural features; on another, identify special challenges that could be turned into opportunities. For instance, note wet areas where existing downspouts carry storm water, or where the land dips or slopes and collects water.

These areas may seem like nothing more than a mowing problem initially, but in time they may come to represent special places to support and grow a distinct palette of plants that thrive only in wet sites.

~ Write about the site. See what adjectives you use and ask yourself how those adjectives or moods might be translated into materials and the built landscape, the garden art. As an example, here's how architects wrote about the character of the landscape to formulate an approach to adding a museum building to Winterthur, an American country estate in northern Delaware developed by Henry Francis du Pont and now open to the public: "There is a very distinct character to this region, what is commonly called the Brandywine Valley. . . . There is a steepness to the hills, a weathering of the buildings, a feeling of heavy foliage in the trees and woods. All this lends itself to broken forms in building" (Winterthur newsletter, Spring 1989).

~ Make abstract sketches of the site to capture the spirit of the landscape—even those who "can't draw" can still do this since it's an exercise meant simply to interpret rather than to accurately document.

~ Take snapshots of what you're starting with and show them to other people. Others may help you feel and observe things or appreciate characteristics you haven't fully realized yourself.

~ Try to determine and document the history of the site for the past two hundred years. What changes has it gone through? What processes have shaped the land and made it what it is today?

And don't be in a hurry. It takes time to get to know a piece of land, just as it takes time to get to know another person, and in the latter case you have the advantage of being able to ask questions to learn about that person's past and values. (Imagine if your land and house could talk—how would they describe themselves and their relationship to their surroundings and to the natural processes that they're a part or a product of?) If you're new to a site, live there a full year—a complete cycle of the seasons—before making any significant changes. What initially may seem like a decrepit old tree may become a special place to witness woodpeckers, or a view to a neighbor's property that's obscured by summer foliage may reveal in the winter a dramatic focal point such as a barn, a pond, a rock outcropping, or a mature oak tree.

America is a land rich in diverse natural beauty, from the rugged peak of Mount Hood in Oregon to the shoreline of Isle au Haut in Maine. The loveliness and wildness of such areas have helped define the spirit of America.

DRAWING FROM AMERICA'S RICH NATURAL HISTORY

The Chinese and Japanese concept of the pleasure garden is largely based on capturing the essence of natural areas. Americans' love affair with Japanese gardens—evidenced by the countless large glossy books published on such gardens—suggests that this principle speaks to our modern-day spiritual needs or our quest for emotional pleasure from our gardens and I believe explains why many homeowners want a Japanese garden. Even after several centuries of clearing and development, America is still a land rich in natural beauty. You don't have to travel far to find places that give pleasure to the senses and uplift the spirit, no matter which part of the country you live in, even major metropolitan areas. It makes little sense to imitate a foreign culture—that is, to emulate an exotic nature—when we have so much lovely native scenery to draw from. The rocks, cliffs, pines, and ponds found in China are different and look different, in some cases dramatically so, from those in Vermont or North Carolina, so if you want to add rocks in your garden, study nearby natural rock outcroppings instead of studying how rocks are placed in Chinese or Japanese gardens. In trying to copy Japanese or Chinese gardens, you would be trying to capture a sense of a place that's not only distant but also remote from your own experience—one you've perhaps never seen nor felt.

Studying natural rock outcroppings may provide lessons on creating rock compositions in a garden.

The balance of rock, water, and plants of a coastal tidal pool may provide inspiration for creating a swimming pool evocative of nature.

The relationship of rocks to water at the edge of a natural pond can inform the naturalistic treatment of a swimming pool edge.

A wet meadow such as this one in Unionville, Pennsylvania, inspired the creation of a "biostream" to handle storm water wisely.

Tidal pools may provide local sources of inspiration for a water feature in a coastal garden; or natural ponds and lakes could offer lessons on how to blend a swimming pool into an inland garden. Natural meadows and prairies may suggest planting patterns for perennial beds. Hedgerows or field edges may quietly model patterns for shrub borders or screening plantings. And the lines, forms, and moods of our natural forests, as beautiful as any on the planet, may provide inspiration and yield lessons to the observant for developing woodland gardens. Whether you're drawn to explore a rocky ledge with water dripping off it or linger in a mossy woodland clearing, recognize the moments in nature that speak to you individually and evaluate why that is so. What is it about them that makes you feel the way you do? Identifying and distilling such places and experiences will be a tool to help you successfully capture the essence of nature in your own garden. So seek out and spend time in local parks near you. Stop and admire or photograph patches of woods, prairie, desert, or beach that you're particularly drawn to. There are endless special moments in nature to interpret into garden art. Look for local inspiration.

REEVALUATING YOUR HORTICULTURAL TRAINING

In some cases capturing the essence of nature may involve overcoming standard horticultural practices or being able to break gardening "rules" we've all been taught. The science, as opposed to the art, of growing plants dominates horticultural education in this county. We're trained not in the aesthetics of nature but rather in how to optimize plant growth and produce perfect specimens, which shouldn't be surprising given that most, if not all, university horticulture departments are in schools of agricultural science, a long way across campus from the art department.

In Japan, with its centuries of gardening tradition and training based on the aesthetics of nature, gardeners learn ways to produce picturesque plants as though mother nature had produced them. To create the impression of a natural stream, for example, gardeners in Japan grow and plant trees at angles to emulate those streamside trees reaching out for light. Moreover, Japanese horticulturists train plants in a variety of other ways with the objective of developing character, in essence prematurely aging a plant. New spring shoots on pine trees are broken in half when they're still tender to stunt the trees' growth, thus making them appear more like picturesque trees growing in the wild. Second- and third-year needles are stripped off pine branches, making the trees appear open and airy like the windblown ones on the mountainsides of Japan. Weights are tied to branches, and branches are also pulled down and tied back to the trunks to accelerate the effects gravity would accomplish in time. Leaf through books on bonsai and you'll see the differences in ideas of beauty and in philosophies and approaches to the art of growing plants between the East and the West.

Our ingrained tendency to space plants an equal distance apart and in neat rows instantly conveys that they were planted by humans. Studying mother nature's plantings, as seen here, and following their example helps bring a sense of nature into gardens and landscapes.

By contrast, horticultural techniques taught and practiced here yield optimal growth rather than the picturesque forms produced by nature. Students are taught to stake and prune trees to grow absolutely straight with an upright trunk, without consideration of the mood or visual effect the end product creates. We plant as though we're putting in fence posts—that is, equally spacing plants in neat rows. Whether we're planting a perennial border or using trees and shrubs to mark boundaries, create privacy, or form a windbreak, we tend to place plants of all equal size an equal distance from one another. These perfectly spaced plants instantly convey that they were planted by human hands, since such patterns rarely occur in nature. You'll need to overcome these planting tendencies if you wish to capture a sense of the wild in your garden. Study how close together mother nature plants trees and you'll likely discover a holly tree sprouting from the base of a beech, or sassafras forming a domed thicket as root suckers spread out from the parent stems and produce trunks mere inches apart. Or in the Southwest, for instance, you'll discover that creosote bush (*Larrea divaricata*) has a distinct distribution pattern—solitary plants widely spaced over the landscape—resulting from its ability to suppress the growth of other plant species by releasing a toxic substance (an ability known as allelopathy).

To emulate nature, you'll have to overcome the countless images and examples of man-made landscapes where plants appear as though they're filling in the boxes of a crossword puzzle. Mix different sizes of shrubs and trees of the same kind. Throw a handful of stones to determine where to plant bulbs to achieve natural-istic patterns. Or study an exact plant population pattern in nature and apply it or adapt it.

ALLOWING NATURAL PROCESSES TO SHAPE YOUR GARDEN

Allowing natural processes to play a hand in your garden is certainly one of the easiest ways to capture the sense of nature. For instance, allow plants to self-seed and use annuals and perennials that do so readily (but not aggressively). This is one of the most satisfying and effective ways early on in the development of a garden to achieve naturalistic planting patterns and population densities similar to those in the wild. In my own garden I scatter seed stalks of money plant (*Lunaria annua*) throughout newly created beds and let the wind, soil, and competition ultimately determine where they germinate and grow. *Verbena bonariensis*, another self-seed-ing annual, finds cracks and niches I never would have imagined on my own. Wine cup (*Callirhoe involucrata*), purple shiso (*Perilla frutescens* var. *purpurascens*), spi-der flower (*Cleome hasslerana*), bronze fennel (*Foeniculum vulgare* 'Purpureum'), and corydalis (*Corydalis* spp.)—a mix of native and exotic species—all have surprised and delighted me with drifts, clumps, and chance sporadic individual plants in my garden as I allow them to grow where they choose for the most part. Every part of the country has self-seeding annuals that can provide this effect and quickly reveal to us the planting patterns of nature. (If you need help to learn about them, call the horticulturist at your nearest botanic garden for suggestions.)

Besides a kind of natural birth in the garden represented by self-sowing plants, death is also a process of nature that, if given space, can yield emotionally powerful and beautiful images. But American gardeners, no doubt because of our larger cul-tural attitudes toward aging and death, are apt to see this process as something to hide, or "clean up" and remove as rapidly as possible from the garden. We tend not to see or appreciate the beauty of a dead tree's skeleton or a stump that's weather-ing and revealing the interior structure of a tree. The brown stems of a dormant grass, the empty seedpods of a milkweed, or the silvered remnants of coneflower all provide texture and substance and perhaps even animation as their stems or seeds move in the winter winds, all of which is more interesting and gratifying than bare mulch in the winter garden (not to mention their ecological benefits). Yet gardeners are generally compulsive about "cleaning up" their gardens and re-placing trees or shrubs that show the first signs of senescence, rarely allowing death or dormancy to be visually prominent.

At the Jenkins Arboretum in Devon, Pennsylvania, lightning struck a specimen tree, knocking the crown out of it and splitting the main trunk into a handful

Allowing death and decay to be part of the garden, as Harland Hand did with this stump on his patch of land in Berkeley, California, is allowing natural processes to play a role.

The weathering stump of a fallen tree in this garden doesn't detract from the beauty. Rather, it reveals the passage of time and something tangible of the cycles of life and death.

Damaged in a storm, a tree in this Connecticut garden fell among the canopies of other trees. The result of the storm damage became a gift, providing a visual frame the gardeners valued and left.

of standing pieces. As the tree died and weathered it became an intriguing naturally produced wood sculpture in the garden. The result dramatically displayed the power of lightning, a natural process we don't have many opportunities to witness. How often do we stop, look, and wonder about the possibility of beauty and interest before cutting down and removing a tree damaged by lightning or wind or old age? Such natural processes may produce plants with a special character or property that in the end represents a gift, serendipity in the garden. The hand of nature is lent in unexpected and unplanned-for ways, but most often we resist the change and resent the "loss," never seeing the possibility of beauty. Our most common response to a dying or dead tree is a knee-jerk reaction of calling the arborist. We think it's far better to remove a declining tree and replace it with a young tree with little character and no sense of age or the passing of time.

In another example, dilapidated orchard trees were appreciated for speaking of a former time, revealing something of the history of the site and providing intriguing elements in the landscape. In a Connecticut garden I visited some years ago, I learned that when the couple bought the old farmstead, the husband wanted to remove all the aging uncared-for trees on the property, including remnant orchard fruit trees, to create a clean slate from which to begin making a garden. The

A decrepit orchard tree might typically be seen as something to clear away and clean up in making a garden. But here the gardener turned it into a unique garden feature by creating a pathway beneath it.

An old orchard tree is incorporated and honored in the garden the late Jane Platt developed on her property in Portland, Oregon.

Polly Hill saw the beauty in this dying tree and left it standing as an archway through the wall opening in her garden (now the Polly Hill Arboretum) on Martha's Vineyard.

At the Betty Ford Alpine Garden in Vail, Colorado, the skeleton of a once-majestic tree adds a sense of sculpture, of time past, and of nature to the garden.

wife, admiring the picturesque nature of these trees as well as the story they told of the passage of time, convinced him to leave them during the clean-up process. On my visit to their garden several years into the process, the most enchanting moment I enjoyed was walking through a living tunnel created by the branches of an old fallen-over orchard tree.

The bleached white skeletons of dead trees standing or lying in natural areas are some of the strongest and most emotionally evocative elements in such landscapes. Our eye naturally goes to them; they are focal points that speak of the climate, of the passage of time, and of birth and death. In her garden on Martha's Vineyard, Polly Hill showed her appreciation of such elements in nature. When a tree, perhaps an eastern red cedar (*Juniperus virginiana*), got shaded out at the edge of her garden and died, she left it standing. Its distinctly arched trunk, perhaps shaped by the shade and snow loads, became silvery in time. For some years it created an intriguing skeletal archway over an opening in a rock wall, its silvery trunk harmonizing with the gray stone.

The gardener who sees the beauty in the unplanned-for event and then embraces it as part of the art or drama of the landscape will likely have an evocative and emotionally resonant garden. While it's hard to plan for unique features in the garden resulting from natural processes, being open to their possibility and pausing to see if there is an opportunity or gift in the result requires little effort—only thought, evaluation, and perhaps a fresh perspective.

RESPECTING THE INDIVIDUAL

Many times gardeners wind up fighting not only natural processes but the natural growth habits of individual plants or the tendencies of a species as well. On a regular basis I've been asked how to grow plants on top of the shallow roots of trees such as beeches or maples. My advice is to not plant anything there at all, but to admire the patterns of the exposed roots and the beauty of the trunk flare. Adding soil to cover the roots or digging into the surface roots not only denies the uniqueness of such trees but also compromises their health.

Or consider the much-used flowering forsythia. When this shrub is allowed to produce its long wandlike branches, which become completely cloaked with yellow flowers in early spring, it's easy to appreciate its grace and understand its popularity as a garden ornamental. But more often than not, these shrubs are sheared into "meatballs," and the charm and unique beauty of forsythia is then utterly sacrificed. Pruning can and should be done to contain the size of trees and shrubs without destroying the unique personality they offer. Think about bonsai, an art form demonstrating this concept. Tree species that normally would reach great heights are pruned to keep them very small, yet they have the look of full-grown, aged specimens. Generally the trick is to avoid quick and easy shearing, and instead to hand prune by thinning so that the basic personality of the plant is preserved while the scale is reduced. So as not to spend countless hours thinning, also think about the ultimate size of the plant when you're placing it and make sure the location is appropriate.

The same tendency shown by home gardeners to struggle against the distinct growing habits of plants is apparent in the plant industry. A look at gardening catalogs reveals endless efforts to produce plants with "improved" forms. Plant breeders work to make tall plants short, delicate petals thick, single flowers double, red flowers blue, flat petals ruffled. They work to make spring-flowering plants repeat bloom in the fall or fertile flowers sterile to last longer. They make plants we love look like other plants; consequently, we have daffodils that look like dahlias, dahlias that look like chrysanthemums, and mums that look like peonies. It seems that we come to take for granted whatever original quality we appreciated in the plant and want to turn it into something else. Capturing nature means appreciating the distinct character not just of the place but also of the individual plants of that place.

APPRECIATING CHANGE IN NATURE

While I was working in Japan with Saburo Sone, a traditional garden maker in Kyoto, I asked him if plant breeders there were developing cherry trees with longer-lasting blooms. I had seen numerous tourists disappointed that they had missed by just a few days the famous weeping cherry trees in bloom at Tenryu-ji, the temple garden where I was working. Certainly, I reasoned, the Japanese who make annual pilgrimages to numerous parks and gardens to see cherries would have a better chance of seeing the fleeting display (and tourism would be enhanced) if the blooms lasted longer. He laughed. Then he explained to me that the Japanese revere the cherry blossom, in part, because of its ephemerality. Its beauty has an intensity because of its fleeting nature. Cherry trees in bloom offer a brief window of opportunity, and one must make an effort if one is going to picnic beneath branches while they are blossom laden. If cherries were to bloom all summer, their special beauty would in effect be lost.

Change is fundamental in nature—it comes with the seasons, more dramatically in some parts of the country than in others. Change occurs daily from morning to night and is noticeable in gardens and plants as life cycles progress through germination, growth, flowering, and fruiting. To appreciate nature is to appreciate change, yet so much in our modern approach to gardening runs counter to this realization. We work hard at minimizing change and, I fear, frequently don't even realize what we're missing out on.

We go to garden centers in the spring to buy six-packs of compact annuals such as marigolds that have been forced into early bloom and bred to stay small. After we plant them in our gardens, they essentially remain unchanged until frost. Their ever-blooming appearance is a constant for nearly half the year. In our quest for deriving greater satisfaction from our gardens, we've lost track of where the satisfaction comes from. Without change, there is little to celebrate, and little to take notice of on a daily basis. Daily and seasonal changes are a big part of the drama nature gives to our landscapes and gardens; we should work to maximize the sense of change if we want to create emotionally evocative gardens.

This is why dwarf conifers and broad-leaved evergreens—constants in the landscape—should be used in moderation or as backdrops to other plants that do change through the seasons. A garden of only dwarf conifers or broad-leaved evergreens will demonstrate little seasonal variation and, at least with the dwarf conifers, subtle growth from one year to the next. Going back to self-sowing annuals, because they provide a different overlay or pattern of plants in the garden from one year to the next, they contribute to the sense of change with little or no effort on the part of the gardener. One year I had a mass of *Cleome* in a new bed; the next year only a few came up in that particular area.

No other plant provides fragrance like a lilac. For those who enjoy its scent, isn't that reason enough to plant this shrub and anticipate those few magical days in April or May when a handful of flower clusters can be picked to sink our nose into to draw a breath of lilac? Or how about the single cold fall day when ginkgos drop all their leaves at once, creating a circular golden carpet? It's a garden event some friends I know anticipate annually by betting on the predicted date. Yet we've come to judge such ephemerality or singular cause for celebration as a liability in a garden plant. We want four seasons of interest, half a year of color, or everlasting foliage from a plant before we devote space to it. We've come to believe we want Christmas everyday in our gardens, when what provides a far greater sense of satisfaction is a rich sequence of distinct celebrations throughout the year, a cycle of constant change.

WORKING WITH WHAT YOU'VE BEEN GIVEN

The old adage for writers is "write about what you know." The gardening version of that is "work with what you've been given" and is another take on how to successfully cultivate a sense of place. Many may protest this notion, arguing that they don't have a shred of nature left to nurture or any character on the site to appreciate—in fact, they're "starting with nothing." But this advice applies even when you have a site deemed most unsuitable for garden making.

The ruins of an industrial gunpowder mill, for instance, wouldn't be an obvious starting point for making a great garden, yet such a site in Wilmington, Delaware, was transformed into a magical landscape with a strong sense of place and serves as an inspiring example of how to apply this principle. On the site of the original Du Pont family home and gunpowder works, Louise du Pont Crowninshield (who grew up at Winterthur, mentioned earlier) and her husband, Francis Boardman Crowninshield, set about making a garden by working with what they found when they moved there in 1923. "Here they set for themselves the ambitious proj-

"Work with what you've been given." This can be done even on the site of industrial ruins, as demonstrated by the Crowninshields, who transformed the remains of the original DuPont Company gunpowder mills in Wilmington, Delaware, into a garden with a strong sense of place and beauty.

ect of transforming this unsightly industrial area into an intriguing and fascinating arrangement of terraced gardens," writes Norman Wilkinson in his 1972 book about the site, which is now known as the Hagley Museum. Wilkinson notes that the Crowninshields acted as their own designers and landscape architects, tearing down most of the mill structures and creating a garden on the foundation walls. Wilkinson goes on to describe the gardens:

> The Crowninshield gardens are an ingenious blending of the formal and the natural, of restored antiquity imposed upon preserved vestiges of the more recent past. Brick-arched tunnels lead to the subterranean furnace remains of the old refinery on top of which beds of flowers blossom in brilliant colors. Huge saltpeter kettles surround brick columns marking the bounds of the old building, dark metallic counterpoints to the sculptured marble figures . . . and a raceway of murmuring water that once brought power to turn the wheels of the mills courses the length of the garden, its stone walls festooned with gnarled wisteria and other clinging vines. . . . Here is an overlay of two Du Pont traditions, the horticultural and the industrial, blended into a truly unusual garden that is most beautiful in the spring of the year. (122, 125)

Consider another example: at the Scott Arboretum, the campus of Swarthmore College, a garden courtyard for a large new academic building was to be developed where a small stone annex building stood. The designers involved in the project drew inspiration from the nondescript building. At first the obsolete structure was to be partially demolished, leaving a ruin in the garden, perhaps similar to the way the Crowninshields had developed their garden decades earlier. Later the planners realized that such a process would have left something structurally unsound, so the building was entirely torn down and the stone salvaged and reused in the design that honored and arose from the original building. The original footprint of the demolished building is completely outlined in the new garden. At some points the reference to the old building is a line of stones flush with the ground, providing an ornamental band through planting beds or a contrast in texture where it runs through smooth flagstone terraced areas. At times it jumps up to serve as a knee-high sitting wall and in other sections it's a full-sized wall with window wells enlarged to serve as sitting nooks. Inside the footprint outline are planting beds, walkways, and a large room of lawn, along with freestanding pillars reminiscent of columns, and beams in the former building that now support vines in the garden. The concept, design, and materials used in the creation of the courtyard garden all arose from what was on the site, what the designers had been given to work with.

As a more general example, rock discovered during construction excavation procedures is rarely regarded with delight or as a gift to work with. It is usually singled out in contracts as cause to spend contingency money for its removal, but

The Cosby Courtyard at the Scott Arboretum of Swarthmore College is an example of "working with what you've been given" to create a sense of place. A small building on the site was demolished and gave rise to this garden design as well as the stone used in the garden structure.

an unexpected rock outcropping may provide an opportunity to create a power-ful place in the garden or, in the example of Fallingwater, could even become the center of a living room floor.

Or more generally still, many gardeners spend an inordinate amount of time, energy, and resources to modify their site, in effect chasing what they don't have, working against what they've been given. Those with shade complain about the difficulty of growing with no sun; those with full sun complain about the harsh sun and plant to create shade; those with "poor drainage" add sand, drains, and whatnot; and those with dry soil feel compelled to add peat and humus or com-plicated irrigation systems. Spending water resources to support lawns and garden plants that require copious water, as homeowners in the arid western states have done for decades, is working against nature and denying the sense of place found there. Instead, what is called for is to discover what one can successfully and appro-priately grow under the given conditions, however much or little average annual rainfall there is, however rocky or sandy the soil, however hot or cold the winters and summers are.

The typical home lot today doesn't start on the ruins of industry or demol-ished buildings, but it has likely been stripped not only of forest or field cover but its very topsoil as well. In such stripped sites where it seems there is "nothing to work with," a sense of place can still come from the site itself, or from the history of the site.

GARDENING BY EDITING AND SIMPLIFICATION

While perhaps the most common experience today is for a new homeowner or garden maker to start with an empty lot—farm fields that have become suburban development—at the other end of the spectrum is the scenario of developing a home on land that hasn't been dramatically altered by human activity. Surely it is the dream of many to acquire such a site. In this scenario, one wants to disturb the land as little as possible in adding the house, to preserve what it was that in-spired acquiring the site in the first place, but the landscape may need to be edited somewhat in order to bring out its natural beauty. As Jens Jensen wrote, garden making as an art form isn't about duplicating nature. It's an artistic expression, an interpretation of nature. Many natural areas are so rich in detail from dense plant growth that there are no discernible patterns or places that we can feel comfort-able with. We need spaces, lines, and forms to read in the landscape so we're not visually confused and emotionally flustered. By selective subtraction, we can make a place in the landscape for ourselves, an invitation to be a part of it. Something as simple as a path through a wood or a meadow—subtracting plants to create a walkway—may be enough to invite us in. By editing or simplification we can em-phasize the special features, plants, or compositions we value, or create moments or experiences to enjoy. Eliminating shrubs to reveal tree trunks; eliminating trees to

An example of "gardening by editing" at the Henry Foundation in Gladwyne, Pennsylvania: with the subtraction of vegetation, a dramatic rock outcropping became a focal point and setting for the display of choice native plants.

Creating a path through a native woodland is an example of gardening by subtraction to create a landscape that invites us in and doesn't overwhelm us with nature's richness.

Removing the roadside weeds of Japanese honeysuckle and multiflora rose allowed the beauty of a stand of sassafras trees to be appreciated—gardening by subtraction.

create a glade to see the sky; removing herbs to expose stones; and removing trees from a lookout point to open a view are all examples of landscape editing with a focus on the sense of place.

An overgrown Delaware hedgerow I used to pass daily at the edge of a property appeared as a tangle of trees, shrubs, and vines, many of which were invasive weeds. Rather than cut the entire lot down, the owner selectively removed much of the underbrush to reveal the unique branching habit of sassafras trees that had been completely obscured. The hedgerow took on an artistic expression of sassafras silhouetted against the pasture behind and provided a visual delight that could be appreciated by any passerby.

In another instance, in a former garden of my own I converted a lawn into a meadow by suspending the mowing. Quickly in the first few years, frost aster and goldenrod grew up in the meadow and bloomed in the fall to make a gratifying display, but exotic thistle, a noxious weed, also sprang up. By selectively weeding out the thistle, I encouraged the meadow to take on the aspect of a huge perennial border, and by annual mowing I kept the trees and shrubs that would naturally regenerate over time from turning the meadow into woods—gardening by subtraction.

At Stan Hywet Hall and Gardens in Akron, Ohio, landscape architect Warren Manning created a great American garden by removing trees to open up vistas through native woods. He took advantage of the American landscape and celebrated the sense of place he found there through a process of editing.

The renowned gardens at Stan Hywet, an Akron, Ohio, estate that is now a public institution, provide several outstanding examples of gardening by editing and simplification on a grander scale. Warren Manning, a prominent landscape architect who ran his own landscape design firm from 1896 until his death in 1938, designed this estate in 1911 for Frank Seiberling, an industrial leader in Akron. In an article in *Landscape Architecture* (1987), Blanche Linden-Ward wrote that they

In another example created at Stan Hywet, gardening by simplification resulted in a vista and walkway radiating from the house composed of a naturalistic allée of birch trees.

Fletcher Steele celebrated the sense of place he discovered at Naumkeag in his design of the Blue Steps, which relies on the beauty of the birch trees he discovered growing on the property.

did not look to a European aristocracy for their model. "Instead," she wrote of their collaboration, "the designer and patron wanted to create a style that reflected American culture's freer, more adaptive, expansive qualities as well as a particular midwestern sense of place" (66).

Originally the site encompassed natural woodland, orchards, fields, pasture, and quarry land, and while the mansion *was* filled with European antiques, Manning used editing versus clearing and recreating European antecedents as the basic strategy for revealing a sense of place. Linden-Ward identified various ways Manning did this. He laid out the serpentine drive to pass through an old apple orchard. For the lawns, he specified various types of grasses to be grown at different heights to further capture the feel of an agrarian past. He relied upon existing American chestnuts supplemented with the planting of other American tree species to define the central space and he opened up dramatic vistas to take advantage of such things as the setting sun and specimen sycamores.

Manning's firm, which was engaged for more than 1700 projects both private and public, made a national reputation by using native plants as the basis for designs. He also provided training for other later landscape architects, including Fletcher Steele. Not surprisingly, designing by subtraction and simplification is evident in the work of Steele as well. At Naumkeag, the garden Steele created in 1938 to 1939 for Mable Choate in Stockbridge, Massachusetts, a stairway known as the Blue Steps, focused on native white-trunked paper birch (*Betula papyrifera*), is reminiscent of Manning's Ohio allée. Set on a steep hillside, the design reveals the essential beauty of birches while clearly being an artistic expression. By simplifying the composition to consist of symmetrically mirrored cascading stairways surrounded by birches that were either preserved or randomly planted in patterns that occur in nature, Steele brings the beauty and growth habit of the birches to our attention and comfortably invites us into the space. In her 1989 book on Fletcher Steele, Robin Karson suggests that the design for the Blue Steps was probably inspired by the native trees on the site and points out that the white railings of the stairs play on the birch trunks.

HONORING THE HISTORICAL AND CULTURAL LAYER

In addition to the natural history of the site, the other equally important dimension to capturing the sense of place is its cultural history. In many instances the expression of humans' past relationship with the land has come to speak about a place as much as or more than its natural features. If a house, building, or garden is to fit appropriately with the site, to be sensitive to the site or have integrity, this dimension must be explored and considered in the design process. Patterns of land use, vernacular architectural styles, and traditional building materials may have evolved for such a long period of time in association with an area that they have come to speak of the region or site.

British gardening guru Gertrude Jekyll made this observation in her 1901 book, *Home and Garden*, with reference to her own country, but in this case the advice travels well:

> I always think it a pity to use in any one place the distinctive methods of another. Every part of the country has its own traditional ways, and if these have in the course of many centuries become 'crystallized' into any particular form we may be sure that there is some good reason for it, and it follows that the attempt to use the ways and methods of some distant place is sure to give an impression as of something uncomfortably exotic, of geographical confusion, of the perhaps right thing in the wrong place. (32)

An image of an adobe-style house in a small town on the East Coast pops into my mind every time I read this passage. Sadly, the image epitomizes the phrase "geographical confusion" to me.

Regional differences in architectural styles and building materials may be the product of climate, topography, and indigenous flora and fauna, but these distinctions also come from the cultural history and values of the immigrants that settled

The human culture found in an area in the past frequently defines the sense of place. The ancient Pueblo cultures of the Southwest helped to "crystallize" certain styles and building materials in that area and continue to shape the appearance of modern buildings, such as those at Sol y Sombra (the last residence of Georgia O'Keeffe) in Santa Fe, New Mexico, and a private modern residence in Mesa, Arizona.

regions. In New England, qualities of austerity and piety persist from the legacy of the Puritans along with architectural styles they brought as immigrants from East Anglia in southeastern England. The saltbox house and the Cape Cod house speak of this part of the country and its cultural history. In the Delaware Valley, Quakers from the North Midlands of England brought values of frugality and function with them, including simplicity in architectural forms made of enduring materials. Stone and brick houses laid out in a straightforward manner referred to as the "four over four plan" (meaning four large rooms laid out on two floors with central hallways) and the "Quaker plan" (three rooms on the first floor with a full second story) became "crystallized" in this region. Quaker meetinghouses lack spires and towers as well as stained glass windows. They appear as humble as a one-room schoolhouse, unlike most buildings designed for religious worship. The plainness in design and honesty in materials from the Quaker heritage is still evident in the region and helps to define its unique character. In the Appalachian region, emigrants who were mostly farmers came from Scotland, Ireland, and northern England with values of independence, self-reliance, and hard work. One-room stone or log cabins built there were similar to those in northern England.

Numerous other groups and cultural influences have shaped the appearance of America: the ancient Pueblo cultures in the Southwest; the Spanish conquistadores who first came to Mexico, bringing with them a Moorish as well as an Iberian heritage, and then influenced the appearance of California, the Southwest, and Florida; the German immigrants in the upper Midwest and the French in Louisiana. Our country expresses a diversity of culturally shaped landscapes that remain unique and tied to certain geographical areas, in spite of the homogenizing effects of television and mass mobility.

One intriguing place to learn about the culturally shaped landscape firsthand is the Frontier Culture Museum in Staunton, Virginia. This open-air museum aims to increase the public's understanding of "the formation of a distinctive American folk culture from the synthesis of European, African, and indigenous peoples," as outlined in the museum's mission statement. An eighteenth-century German farm, a mid-nineteenth-century Scotch-Irish farm, a seventeenth-century English farm, and a nineteenth-century American farm have all been painstakingly dismantled, moved, and rebuilt at the museum to show how the various cultural influences and backgrounds of immigrants helped shape the look of America. A cultural history has been reflected in our landscape and defines our relationship to the land since gardening first began here. It is this cultural history that makes the terra-cotta tiles of Californian mission buildings and gardens feel not quite right in New England and the saltbox-inspired garden shed look ill at ease in a Texas suburb. Thus gaining a knowledge and awareness of the cultural history of a site is also fundamental to capturing a sense of place.

Look at your home property: is there anything that reveals the region where it is? If so, you've captured or preserved the sense of place. If not, consider this passage from James Michener's *Iberia* (1968) to evaluate a sense of place:

Having completed a rapid survey of the plaza, I closed my eyes and asked, "Is there anything here that would prove I am in Spain?" I looked again, and apart from the obvious signs in Spanish, saw nothing that would betray the origin of this city. It could have been Italy, or southern France, or even rural Texas. I want to make this point secure because travelers often expect strange cities to look a certain way, but with modern technology, architecture, and traffic, most of them look alike. If I had tried this test of "Where am I?" in the plazas of the villages and towns of southern Extremadura the answer would have been, "This can only be Spain," but the cities no. They were international. (47)

I contend that for your garden to provide a deep sense of satisfaction, when you close your eyes, visualize it, and ask, "Where am I?" the answer can only be the place from which it was made.

2

Derive Beauty from Function

To make our home gardens and man-made landscapes practical—so they support our pattern of living—many things need to be associated with them. That probably means a driveway and a place to park cars, a mailbox, a place for firewood if we have a fireplace or woodstove, a place for the dog to exercise or the kids to play if we have those, an area for garbage cans, things for cooking outside and eating outside, and maybe a place to dip into cool water or relax in hot water. These elements are generally treated as if they're outside of the garden itself, not an integral part of it, when in fact they offer opportunities to provide not only functionality to our home properties but also beauty to our gardens and living experience. If we appreciate them as opportunities, we will develop deeply satisfying gardens and landscapes with integrity. This, then, is the second principle: derive beauty from function.

Applying this principle creates integrity in the garden, similar to the integrity in architecture that Frank Lloyd Wright talked about. Integrity in the garden comes from making the landscape function well; designing for that will result in inspiration for the appearance of the garden.

THE PITFALLS OF ORNAMENTATION WITHOUT FUNCTION

Going to a garden center to buy "ornaments" to beautify the garden results in a garden full of stuff, mostly kitschy stuff at that, not beauty or an integrated sense of design from purposeful living. We overlook the opportunities the mundane but necessary articles offer for adding beauty. A property may be devoid of statues, sculpture, and other such ornamentation yet still have an elegance if the functional elements are genuine in materials and gracefully fulfill their function. Don't compromise on the essentials in pursuit of fluff—dressing up with nonessentials. This holds true both inside and outside of the house. To help illustrate this principle, let me draw from my experiences in Japan again.

In Japanese gardens, articles such as stone lanterns and washbasins, though frequently described as "ornaments" by Westerners, didn't start out simply as ornamental additions to a garden. They had a reason for being in the garden; they served a purpose. Stone lanterns were the light fixtures of ancient Japan. At shrines they lit walkways and grounds for evening festivities and ceremonies, and later they were added to gardens to serve the same purpose. Their placement, size, and shape were largely determined by what they were intended to illuminate. They were not set in gardens willy-nilly solely for their intrinsic beauty. Tall lanterns have a rock at their base not as an ornament but to serve as a step so someone could physically reach the light box and put a candle or oil lamp in it. To hold the fire source in the light box, lanterns need to be level; consequently, they don't look right if they're positioned at an angle. And lanterns developed an association with washbasins since those were areas of activity where illumination would be helpful. Thus, these characteristics and associations based on practicality have ultimately shaped the aesthetic in Japanese gardens.

Washbasins, also originally associated with Japanese shrines, have evolved in a fashion similar to stone lanterns. Found at the entrances of centuries-old shrines in Japan, these basins served the purpose of allowing visitors to rinse their hands before proceeding to the shrine itself, which had perhaps symbolic as well as practical value. They became an essential element in the Japanese tea garden, a place where guests ritualistically rinsed their hands before entering the teahouse to participate in a tea ceremony, again both a physical action and a symbolic gesture that mentally prepared the guests for the experience of the tea ceremony. The basin's location and relationship to other elements in the tea garden was thus determined by a prescribed sequence of experiences or movement through the garden and not just based on aesthetic judgments.

Accounts written by early tea masters describe how stepping-stones, another integral part of the tea garden, were originally added for the primary purpose of keeping visitors out of the mud. The writings of the next generation of tea masters suggest that it's the aesthetic value first and the practical function second that should determine their placement in the garden. In modern Japan, after hundreds of years of garden evolution, there are stepping-stone paths in gardens that are meant only to be looked at as part of a garden picture, even though they could allow visitors a means to pass through the garden. In these instances they provide an imagined journey.

Scarecrows in Japanese gardens were based on the idea that sound would scare away wild animals. A cut section of bamboo would be balanced like a seesaw on a stand, with one end sliced at an angle and placed in such a way as to capture water dripping into it. Once the open end was full of water, it would become top-heavy and then tip, allowing the water to run out. The now-empty piece of bamboo would swing back upright and its lower end would hit a rock strategically placed directly under it. The repeated bonking sound created by the bamboo filling and then emptying chased undesired animals from the area. Like washbasins and lanterns, scarecrows are part of modern Japanese gardens today more for their beauty than due to the need to chase away animals. They appear as beautiful water features, with the sound adding a melancholy feel to the garden and their movement adding animation.

While the original function of lanterns, washbasins, stepping-stones, and bamboo scarecrows is now obsolete and they appear in modern Japanese gardens solely as ornamental objects, their original purpose still determines their placement and dictates their treatment. And when their function is honored, they maintain integrity, a genuine quality, a beauty. It makes them look and feel right in the garden. On the other hand, Westerners who relate to these artifacts as ornaments or sculpture without appreciation for their function may wind up placing them randomly in gardens. The effect is like putting on a name tag upside down because it's in a language you can't read—it doesn't communicate your name and it certainly doesn't look right to anyone who can read the language.

This same evolution of a functional object toward an ornamental object has happened with articles we're thoroughly familiar with in American architecture and landscapes. Think about window shutters for a moment. Shutters on houses originally provided protection. Placed on hinges, they could easily be pulled into a closed position over openings or glass windows. They looked the way they did because of the function they provided. Today on countless modern "McMansions" we see the suggestion of shutters as plastic plaques simulating wood boards permanently affixed to the sides of windows. They can't move; there's not even a suggestion of a hinge; they serve no function. They are superficial ornamentation and vestiges of shutters. No longer genuine or useful, they have lost any sense of integrity and of beauty as a result. The ultimate useless "shutter" is the foot-wide plaque on the outside of a window that's four or five feet across. Even if they could close, they wouldn't cover the window opening. Adding such panels on the outside of a house in imitation of the look, not realizing the purpose these originally served and so not following the dictates for their placement, results only in lessening the integrity of the property.

Even articles that could be regarded as necessary evils in the garden, such as winter protection for plants, can become objects of beauty and ornament in the practice of this principle. Pine trees in Japanese gardens appear to be decorated for some festival with umbrella-like structures of straw rope erected over them as a means of preventing heavy snow loads from accumulating on their boughs and breaking their branches. Temperature-sensitive cycads are cloaked in fanciful straw constructions finished off with black twine and skillfully tied knots. Whether or not it snows, these creations are attractive and don't detract from the overall beauty of the garden, and in fact add winter interest.

Because we haven't yet broadly embraced this principle, our typical approach to winter protection in this country is strikingly different. White styrofoam cones covering rosebushes look like giant upside-down egg cartons. Seeing these all winter long in midwestern gardens made me swear off ever wanting to grow roses. I've seen plants shrouded in garbage bags and corralled in wooden boxes all winter, and these approaches don't add beauty to the garden either. Sadly, numerous examples of winter protection practiced in both private and public gardens in the United States reveal that we have much to learn about seizing opportunities to derive beauty from function.

So rather than import Japanese lanterns or English staddle stones (bases for stacks of hay or straw in old England)—beautiful though they are—or any number of other ornaments or objects from foreign lands that have little or no relationship to our cultural heritage or current lifestyle, first consider the objects and the needs outlined here as obvious opportunities for adding beauty.

FENCES AND WALLS

Fences and walls have been a part of man-made landscapes—whether in Japan, Europe, or the United States—for a long time. In many scenarios they originally provided the important functions of containing livestock, keeping out wild animals or trespassers, or defining ownership. Today we still largely depend upon fences and walls to provide such functions, but they may now also preserve privacy or hide distracting encroachment or development from the viewer in a garden. Fences appear in seminal American literature, expressing their importance in our culture. Recall the story of Tom Sawyer's white washing a fence and the advice Robert Frost gives about fences and neighbors. An article in the *New York Times* titled "Our Land of Fences" (Giovannini 1987) put it this way, "Traditionally designed to keep people or animals in or out, or to mark boundaries and establish territory, fences today have gone beyond the purely functional." In modern America, fences may not be relied upon to mark boundaries or contain livestock as much as to be symbols of the past and of a place.

Travel around the country today and you see forms of fences and walls that have become part of a region's unique aesthetic beauty and cultural heritage. Take the zigzag split-rail fences found on the steep and rocky hills of Virginia and West Virginia. Their building method is a result of the varied topography and the impossibility of sinking a post upright into rocky ground. The form grew in time to be appreciated as a beautiful pattern and so is repeated in suburban properties today, more for its beauty than its function. The old rock walls on Martha's Vineyard provided the same function as the split-rail fences of West Virginia, but they give the island a distinct appearance and are being protected because of their aesthetic and cultural contribution to the landscape, the sense of place they help define. The beautiful Scotch-Irish stone walls around Lexington, Kentucky, are being preserved and even rebuilt by a conservation organization because of their unique beauty and their cultural and historical significance. The old adobe walls along Canyon Road in Santa Fe enclose and protect spaces and privacy today in a distinctly southwestern way, inspiring tourists to travel there to admire and experience their unique beauty.

These styles of fences and walls are all examples of using readily available materials and responding to the challenges of topography or environment. Because of that, they have come to symbolize or capture the distinct character of a region; they fit a locale or capture a specific place while they serve a purpose.

A screen provides protection and privacy as well as ethereal beauty in a private garden in Nutley, New Jersey.

A fence in Edgartown on Martha's Vineyard helps define a unique sense of place.

The wall in Linda Cochran's garden on Bainbridge Island, Washington, encloses and contains the garden while being an integral part of the color composition.

In a Berkeley, California, garden, a simple picket fence subtly harmonizes with the shingle-style house, allowing *Crocosmia* to be the star of the garden in the summer.

In Albuquerque, New Mexico, an automatic gate provides security and enclosure while at the same time not hiding or detracting from the southwestern architecture.

A stone wall in upstate New York at the edge of a farm field was clearly built with both beauty and utility in mind.

The stone walls on Martha's Vineyard have a lacey quality to them despite the weight of the stone, due to their manner of construction, and are a treasured element in the landscape.

This stone wall provides an exquisitely beautiful way to enclose, contain, and define a boundary in Centerville, Delaware.

The zigzag split-rail fences characteristic of Virginia and West Virginia are able to define and enclose spaces even on rocky, steeply hilly terrain. The pattern they create is beautiful but disappearing.

The adobe walls of the Southwest, here in Phoenix, Arizona, in olden days helped to keep livestock in or out, while in modern times they help preserve pleasing views in a rapidly developing region of the country.

A traditional patterned farm fence and gate becomes a sculptural element in the borders developed by André Viette at his perennial nursery in Virginia.

A modern partition screens a property in Nutley, New Jersey, from close neighbors.

DRIVEWAYS AND CAR PARKS

The automobile has dramatically shaped the look of America. The country is laced with an extensive system of multilane highways and dotted with ubiquitous parking lots, some the size of midwestern cornfields. The car has shaped the layout and look of the typical American home property as well, with three-door garages and corresponding blacktop paving or concrete. Accommodations for cars often become the most prominent visual feature of our homes besides the house itself, yet rarely does this need result in something to admire. We tend to think of the driveway as outside the garden, something separate, and the garage, even when it's not a separate structure, somehow doesn't rate as truly a part of the house. It's as though the garden starts at the end of the driveway but doesn't include it; the home starts after you pass through the garage door into the house.

Driveways can be works of art and integral to the garden. Consider the driveway at a residence in Pasadena, California, designed by Charles and Henry Greene, two brothers who led the Arts and Crafts design movement in that region. With orange brick for the two tire tracks and natural stone for the center band, the driveway contains various contrasts and thus visual interest. The color contrast between the orange and the gray is perhaps the most obvious, but there is also a contrast in shape—the rectangles of the brick and the circular forms of the stone—and a contrast in formality—the man-made brick and the stone shaped by nature. This driveway provides the one open view into the property, so it creates the first impression, which is one of beauty because of the design and materials used. It certainly isn't a view you want to look away from or hide. As a driveway, it is still simple, and fully functional.

In other examples where driveways have been treated as opportunities to create beauty, the drive has been incorporated into the overall design of the property in such a way that it's hard to tell whether the drive is in fact a terrace or plaza, a patio, or an extension of the lawn. If a driveway is treated as a garden path with perennial or mixed borders planted along its sides, it doubles as a garden walkway when cars aren't present. The use of bricks, stones, pavers, pea gravel, or a mix of such materials common in garden paths further generates the feeling and creates the appearance that the driveway is also a garden pathway. Even on a small urban plot, the visual impact of a driveway can be minimized if the middle strip is planted as a rock garden. All these approaches to the driveway illustrate how it can be cause for admiration rather than apologies.

At the end of many driveways stands a garage, and for many residences, the garage represents the second largest "garden ornament," to my way of thinking, after the house, if it's a separate structure. We tend to treat garages, just like driveways, as though they lie outside the bounds of the garden, but we thereby miss the opportunity they offer to create interest and add beauty in the landscape or to positively define or divide garden spaces. An attractive side of a garage can create a handsome backdrop to show off a perennial border or provide a sense of privacy for an outside sitting area.

A driveway serves as a work of art on a Pasadena, California, property designed by Charles and Henry Greene in the early 1900s.

Graeme Hardie didn't miss the opportunity to have his garage add to his intimate suburban garden in Nutley, New Jersey. One side of his garage essentially forms the back wall of the garden behind his house, so it would figure prominently in the composition regardless of the treatment. Hardie added an overhang supported by columns to this side of the garage, giving a sense of depth to the structure's side façade and creating the ambience of a porch, say of a garden cottage or guesthouse. The garage breezeway adds an invitation to stroll there and look back at the garden from another vantage point.

In a small urban Charleston, South Carolina, garden, the parking pad functions as a garden patio when not parked in.

Another parking space doubles as a patio in a Charleston, South Carolina, garden.

In a Chestertown, Maryland, garden, a parking place for two creates an inviting entrance to the property and with its lawn seamlessly connects to the garden lawns.

A parking space in Berkeley, California, doubles as a rock garden and perennial border.

The driveway in this California garden serves as an entry plaza but will accommodate guest parking if need be.

A service drive at Grounds for Sculpture in Hamilton, New Jersey, is an integral part of a courtyard displaying sculpture. With this treatment, the drive is a strong part of the overall artful effect.

With a clean design and simple materials, the driveway and garage on this Chestertown, Maryland, property make a positive first impression.

The cobblestone driveway to this New York property is indistinguishable from the front walkway.

At Graeme Hardie's garden in Nutley, New Jersey, the driveway takes on the personality of a garden pathway when cars are absent due to the materials used and the mixed border plantings softening its edges.

At the Elisabeth Carey Miller Botanical Garden in Seattle, Washington, the driveway has much in common with a garden walkway due to the treatment of the paving.

A pea gravel driveway in Cold Spring, New York, is also the entrance path to the front door, and the garage adds interest to the roofline of the house.

At Silas Monsieur's garden in Nutley, New Jersey, the driveway is a welcoming garden feature due to the cobblestones and the pattern used in laying them.

A garage-toolshed at Chanticleer, a former estate in Wayne, Pennsylvania, now open to the public, doesn't take away from the beauty of the gardens.

This functioning garage and workspace at French Farm, a private garden in Greenwich, Connecticut, offers its own charm.

A garage takes on the appearance of a garden pavilion with the addition of columns in Graeme Hardie's Nutley, New Jersey, garden.

BARBECUES AND ALFRESCO DINING

Cooking and eating outdoors is certainly part of the all-American lifestyle, and space designed for this activity in the home garden can serve homeowners well. Making this aspect pleasing to look at, even during the seasons when the weather is inhospitable outside, can turn it into part of the garden art as well.

The so-called council rings that Jens Jensen built into his landscapes are a celebrated and emulated example of designing and providing an area for a fire and socializing. Simple yet elegant, a stone bench in the form of a three-quarters circle creates a space equivalent to the hearth in the home. Such intimate spaces became the heart of his gardens, in much the same way that rustic stone fireplaces provide an interior focus in Frank Lloyd Wright houses. Photographs of Jensen's council rings taken when devoid of fires, cooking, eating, or people are still visually compelling. These broken rings don't need to be in use to be beautiful to look at.

This council ring in Chicago's Columbus Park was part of Jens Jensen's original design, much of which has been restored.

Even an inexpensive grill can be integrated into a garden in a way that offers beauty and preserves integrity.

This permanent grill fixture doesn't take away from the beauty of the garden when it's not in use.

Here are some other examples of attractive and appropriate outdoor places in gardens for cooking and eating that I've admired:

~ Nurseryman Paul Babikow in his home garden created a fire pit in a stone terrace and suspended a grill over it by using a large metal tripod. His design is as pleasing to look at as a piece of sculpture when not in use, which is important given that it's in a spot close to the house where it can be seen in all seasons, even when he and his family members don't venture out into the garden very far.

~ Carlton Goff in his Rhode Island garden created an open-sided pavilion of rough-hewn timbers supporting a slate roof and a central fireplace. Because of the materials used and the proportions of the space, it blends with the garden in all seasons, and it too is a beautiful focal point when not in use.

~ At the Polly Hill Arboretum on Martha's Vineyard, a stone hearth created near the sheep barn provided an outside fixture for cooking while its rustic character blended with that of the rest of the property. Today it's difficult to discern whether it supported the rearing of lambs or the rearing of children, its fit is so natural.

~ In a garden in Northeast Harbor, Maine, the smallest Weber grill, which retails for $39.95, was set up on supporting blocks of rough Maine granite in a pea gravel driveway just outside the back door. The small black shiny pod of a grill and the chunks of stone that held it and raised it to a level for easy burger flipping exhibited some of the same kinds of contrasts found in the Greene and Greene driveway described earlier. With the whole grill very easily removed and stored inside for the winter, the remaining stone pillars would resemble perhaps remnants of hitching posts, and they could serve as quiet markers of the driveway's edge during heavy snowfalls.

~ In a model home garden at a garden show in Germany, a small rectilinear grill was surrounded by a naturalistic grouping of boulders interplanted with ornamental grasses. The boulders could serve as perches to set food platters and utensils on while cooking, and when the grill wasn't in use the boulders and plantings hid the direct view of it from the sitting area of the small garden and disguised the cooking area as a part of the garden in the view from the house.

FURNITURE

For many gardeners with busy lifestyles and multiple demands on time, the teak garden bench and the Adirondack lawn chair have evolved into purely ornamental objects—after all, who has the time to actually sit down and just look at the garden? But furniture is still found in most gardens—small or large, humble or grand—to provide a place to sit. Even if we rarely take the time to linger on a bench or sunbathe on a recliner, their presence in the garden or landscape provides a focal point for our eyes and our emotions. Just seeing the Adirondack chair under the shade of a tree provides the momentary pleasure of imagining its use. We look at it as we go about our tasks or pass by, and enjoy not just the lines of the chair but also its invitation to us to become a part of the garden.

Numerous catalogs offer outdoor furniture in handsome designs made of attractive long-lasting woods or metals. It's now easy to find furniture that looks like high-style art for the sophisticated urban garden or has a rustic character to blend with a rural country cottage. The various examples of garden furniture described in the following paragraphs epitomize the principle of deriving beauty from function.

At Dumbarton Oaks in Washington, D.C., a bench becomes an ornament as well due to its design and careful siting.

A bench designed by Robert and Barbara Tiffany that doesn't need to be sat in to be enjoyed for what it adds to the garden.

In the garden at Dumbarton Oaks in Washington, D.C., which was designed by Beatrix Farrand as a private garden and is now a public garden, a bench set against a stone wall has a high backrest reminiscent of the fancy headboard of a bed frame. *Forsythia suspensa* cascades over the wall from the garden bed above, creating a floral canopy over the bench when in bloom and a leafy one the rest of the growing season. The bench, firmly planted on level ground and protected with the wall behind, makes an inviting and secure place to sit; but even if one doesn't pause on the bench, it's pleasing to look at because of its ornamental quality and the careful garden composition of which it's an integral part.

A unique bench designed by professional furniture designers Barbara and Robert Tiffany of Point Pleasant, Pennsylvania, is composed of scores of sinuous spindles, each curved in such a way that it is part leg, part seat, and part back, and strung together with small spacers between the spindles. The many spindle legs resemble the undulating legs of a millipede. The bench is indeed a piece of wooden sculpture, gracing their own garden with an example of their furniture design work.

At Sol y Sombra, once the home of Georgia O'Keeffe in Santa Fe, oversized, heavy chairs composed of naturalistic chunks of wood grace the garden. Each

Furniture can also subtly provide a place to sit without competing with the garden and its plantings, as in this example in the garden of Silas Monsieur in Nutley, New Jersey.

chair is made up of individual pieces of wood, reminding me of the sun-bleached animal bones O'Keeffe so famously painted, that fit together like a three-dimensional jigsaw puzzle. These chairs can accommodate a body very comfortably, their size and heavy structure encouraging complete relaxation, but with or without bodies in them, the chairs have become sculptural pieces in the garden.

At the Minneapolis Sculpture Garden, a bench made of a thick slab of wood sandwiched between two boulders like mismatched bookends clearly doubles as a work of art and is exhibited as sculpture. When I saw it, a couple, she with her head in his lap, had obviously found its form inviting and were enjoying its usefulness. Its sensual character and lack of backrest perhaps helped inspire their pose.

At Chanticleer in Wayne, Pennsylvania, in the public pleasure garden created from the private estate of Christine and Adolf Rosengarten, the furniture is sometimes painted to echo a color in the surrounding garden. For example, a bright yellow wooden chair plays partners with a 'Sunburst' honey locust in a distant border.

At Grounds for Sculpture in Hamilton, New Jersey, picnic tables have been set in a fluid pattern of connected gravel patches. Consequently there are no puddles beneath the tables, no ugly warn-out turf areas from the concentrated foot traffic.

These stools of carved wood provide a place to sit and also add interest to this garden vignette.

At Grounds for Sculpture the furniture is also sculpture.

The picnic area at Grounds for Sculpture accommodates heavy foot traffic in an aesthetically pleasing way.

The lines and shadows of this chaise longue add artistry to a small patio in a Woodside, California, garden.

Chairs serve as focal points in the Terry Shane Teaching Garden at the Scott Arboretum.

Instead, the artistic composition—a play between gravel and turf and tables—can be displayed without apology and without compromising the overall beauty of the grounds. When the tables are not in use, the area appears to draw inspiration from a Japanese moss and gravel garden; with the tables stored for winter, that would appear to be even more the case.

These examples show that furniture can be of many moods and materials and be pleasing to look at whether or not its intended use is being realized.

CLOTHESLINES

While visiting Jan Moss's garden on Cranberry Island in Maine, I caught a glimpse of a piece of twig art through an opening in a lattice trellis into an area beyond. I thought I was peering into a secret garden. Only after noticing green cord stretching to another similar twig sculpture did I realize that I was looking at an old-fashioned clothesline strung between the two twig end posts. Thus the clothesline provided utility without taking anything away from the charming seaside garden. Much like driveways, clotheslines are rarely thought of as part of the garden, let alone something that could lend beauty to a garden view or composition.

In many developments, building covenants prohibit clotheslines as well as the drying of clothes that could be seen by others. This seems foolish given our excessive energy consumption and the ecological savings that can be realized by air-drying clothing. Learning to see the beauty of clotheslines in the landscape could be a matter of national energy policy.

Legal restrictions aside, where space is tight gardeners particularly loathe giving up area to utility from their small Eden, but in such instances retractable clotheslines could be run above perennial borders. With this approach, the clotheslines might not lend beauty in themselves, but depending on the colors of your laundry, drying clothes might provide a temporary play on the colors of plants in bloom, much like the painted garden furniture at Chanticleer. (A word of caution: when you start buying boxers or bras to match your garden's colors, perhaps you've carried this principle far enough!)

Clotheslines don't have to feel like an imposition in a garden, and depending on the clothes being dried, many even add temporary color that accentuates plants in the garden, as here in Downingtown, Pennsylvania.

An ornamental clothesline in Jan Moss's garden on Cranberry Island, Maine.

The clothesline at the Polly Hill Arboretum on Martha's Vineyard seems to be imitating the layers of flowers on the Chinese dogwood beyond.

COMPOST PILES

Composting is a worthy process to allocate space to, even on small properties, but how many do? And those who make the attempt frequently put an undersized compost bin in the back corner of their backyard and treat it as though they wish it had a trapdoor under it rather than as part of a process that produces "black gold." For a composting operation to succeed, the area allocated to it needs to be designed so the pile is easy to get to and add garden refuse to, easy to mix and turn to speed the process, and easy to retrieve compost from to add back into the garden. The end product is such a valuable commodity for good gardening, it should be given primary consideration rather than tucked in as an afterthought. Granted, it's a process and activity based on refuse and decay, but that doesn't mean it has to be banished for the sake of preserving beauty.

Dan McNeal in his small Downingtown, Pennsylvania, garden used spent sunflower stalks with branches and blades of ornamental grasses woven through them to create a compost bin from the garden itself. The environmentally friendly ephemeral composition changed through the growing season, providing amusement and awareness of the process before the finished compost was ready to feed back into the garden.

These compost bins at the edge of a driveway are easy to access and at the same time help block the view of parked cars from the garden.

Dan McNeal created a compost bin like a basket woven from spent garden material. It became a temporary art form in his Downingtown, Pennsylvania, garden.

In another example, in an Arden, Delaware, suburban garden, more typical and durable composting bins made of wooden lath were placed at the end of the driveway in full view. Thus the bins were easily accessible by garden carts and wheelbarrows. Flower boxes suspended from their sides filled with cascading geraniums transformed the structures into a floral display when viewed from the driveway and from the garden. The bins doubled as a privacy fence, helping to block the view from the garden of vehicles parked in the drive.

On a larger scale, in his garden created from a former dairy farm in Rheinhold, Pennsylvania, Richard Bitner constructed three stone stalls for composting behind

At Montrose in Hillsborough, North Carolina, eastern red cedar logs with bark intact form compost bins; despite their volume, the structures blend unobtrusively into the landscape.

Richard Bitner added stone bays for composting behind the former dairy barn, in keeping with the rural farm character of his property.

the dairy barn, which he uses to store garden equipment. Their character is so in keeping with the barn that they look as though they've always been part of the farming operation, even though they've never processed stall straw or manure.

Nancy Goodwin, at the garden she developed known as Montrose, now open to the public, in Hillsborough, North Carolina, created large square enclosures by stacking eastern red cedar trunks one upon another, much like building a rustic log cabin without doors or windows or a roof. Not only could these structures economically and adequately accommodate large quantities of leaves and weeds from a multi-acre garden, they could be dismantled when the compost was ready to be used and also disassembled and reassembled as the garden grew and changed.

MAILBOXES

Whenever I see a blue mailbox I wonder if the resident was inspired by Taj Mahal's song proclaiming "I'm going to move out to the country and paint my mailbox blue." Because of those lyrics, a blue box symbolizes country living to me, whether this symbolism is intended or not. Like the architecture of a house, the appearance of these small houses for mail can and does convey a sense of place, or a mood, or even an attitude if painted blue.

Postal regulations for mailboxes must be honored to maintain their function, and in some regions and situations maintaining a functional mailbox poses additional challenges. Mailboxes may need to be able to withstand drive-by bashers; or a mailbox may need to be on an adjustable board so it can be extended nearer to the road in order to be accessible after the snowplow has created a snowbank in front of it. These demands dictate design and form, but they may also be handled in such a way as to lend beauty.

The irregular gray stone used in a California garden was carried out to the mailbox by setting the box in a column made of the same material. The gray leaves and purple flowers of lavender planted in a sweep around it softened the stone and complemented the shades of gray. In front of another California property containing a modern house of glass and steel with clean stark lines, a steel arch containing and protecting the mailbox painted a brownish-maroon matched the surrounding ruby-colored *Pennisetum* and carried the clean style of the property all the way to the curb.

TOOLSHEDS

With a bit of luck and imagination, old outhouses, springhouses, smokehouses, or other now-obsolete structures can be scavenged, saved, and converted into toolhouses or garden sheds. Failing to find an old building, one can still creatively design a storage structure to become a focal point and make a positive contribu-

A mailbox in Albuquerque, New Mexico, conveys a special mood.

In Lafayette, California, protecting this mailbox well doesn't take away from the beauty of the curbside view of the garden.

This mailbox structure, with its curved lines and harmonizing color, partners nicely with the *Pennisetum* surrounding it.

tion to the spirit of the garden. For example, Yvonne England at her country herb farm and garden had a two-seater outhouse recreated to provide a structure for storage that complemented the farmhouse, which would originally have had an outhouse. The cookie-cutter miniaturized barns with their fake shutters popping up in backyards across America miss the mark. Real barns, former carriage houses, farm implement sheds, even corncribs can readily be converted to garages, mower sheds, and garden toolsheds while keeping a piece of American vernacular architecture in the garden as it goes from rural landscape to subdivision.

SWIMMING POOLS AND HOT TUBS

While arguably nonessential, swimming pools and hot tubs can be designed and sited so that they function well but are also integrated with the garden. Making them readily accessible from the house while preventing them from being an eyesore to look at all winter from inside becomes part of the challenge, particularly if they're covered and not useable during the winter. They can be treated in a variety of ways for pleasing visual effect without having them look and feel like a giant Caribbean tub dropped into the garden.

Paint the interior of a swimming pool gray or black instead of white and it will immediately resemble more closely the color of lakes, ponds, or tidal pools in the vicinity; thus it will appear as though it belongs there. And how many rectangular bodies of water have you seen in the wild? Pools shaped like a naturally occurring body of water will seem at home in the landscape instead of imposed upon it. Planting beds near the edge of a swimming pool can soften the edges and visually and materially connect the pool to the garden. Diving platforms composed of boulders or resembling fishing piers or docks create the feeling of a natural swimming or fishing hole.

Imitating natural bodies of water isn't the only way to make swimming pools blend into a garden. They can also be incorporated into formal or modern gardens by designing them to appear as an ornamental fountain or water feature while still effectively functioning as a swimming pool. For example, at Mount Cuba Center, a public garden created from the former private estate of Mr. and Mrs. Lammot du Pont Copeland in northern Delaware, a plunge pool designed by Marian Coffin and added in the 1950s is referred to as the Round Garden. The pool itself is in the shape of a Maltese cross with a wide band of coping. Underwater steps face each other on two arms of the cross, while thin jets of water arch from the notches of the arms to meet in the center of the pool. The pool is set in a slight bowl circled by a brick walkway, which in turn is circled by crescent-shaped flower beds. The beds, edged with clipped low hedges, feature a changing display of flowers starting with pansies in the spring, followed by delphiniums in the summer and chrysanthemums in the fall. The Round Garden, then, is a fountain and flower garden to walk through when it's not serving as a dipping pool. Its look is so ornamental, visitors may not even realize the pool was designed for cooling off.

The plunge pool at Mount Cuba, surrounded by mixed beds and formal hedges, serves as an ornamental water feature when not in use by bathers.

While I long to add a hot tub to my own small urban garden, the big boxy hot tubs with bright fiberglass liners offered at every home improvement center strike me as nearly impossible to successfully integrate into a small garden. When the time (or I should say money) comes, I will opt for a round wooden tub that reminds me of a Japanese bathtub or *ofuro*. Its wood, perhaps western red cedar, will naturally weather to ultimately blend gently with the tones of my garden. In the nearby garden with just such a hot tub that inspired my vision, stone and brick steps that spiral around the curved side of the tub not only provide a means to get into and out of the tub but also successfully link the tub to the garden by featuring the same materials as those used in the garden pathways.

Graeme Hardie in his Nutley, New Jersey, garden took another approach to making sure the hot tub doesn't visually dominate a small suburban garden. He built the tub below a garden deck or platform along a walkway through his gently sloping property, taking advantage of the grade change to hide the tub underneath the deck. When not in use, the tub is perfectly covered by a lid attached by piano hinges that completes the slatted wood deck. Most visitors to the garden don't realize a hot tub is there as they walk over it. When the lid is lifted and the tub is in use, the remaining portion of the deck provides a platform for getting into and out of the tub. The necessary equipment to operate the hot tub is also neatly contained and hidden beneath the deck.

A simple wooden hot tub adds charm and warmth to a Media, Pennsylvania, garden.

A hot tub artistically set in a rock composition in a Pennsylvania garden is invisible to visitors passing by at the lower elevations.

Beneath this deck a hot tub is hidden from view when not in use in Graeme Hardie's Nutley, New Jersey, garden.

CELLAR DOORS

In the Midwest today, cellar doors may symbolize the entrance to a safe haven away from tornadoes more than the entrance to a food storage space, but they can also add beauty to a landscape. The doors into the cellar of Silas Monsieur's home in Nutley, New Jersey, are clearly visible to anyone driving into the property. They face the driveway next to the side door of the house and are part of the everyday view of the garden, summer or winter. No doubt because of their prominence, he has made them unusually pleasing to behold; the artistic doors display leaf impressions all over their surface.

GARDEN HOSES

Something as small and seemingly insignificant as a garden hose can have a big presence in the garden. I've visited many great gardens and felt I couldn't fully appreciate their beauty because a bright garden hose had been left sprawled out across a walkway or lying on the lawn. Today finding ways to beautifully yet conveniently store the hose is relatively easy with gardening catalogs offering such devices as large ceramic bowls to coil hoses into. With a hole on the lower side making it easy to leave the hose hooked up to the spigot, such containers provide attractive storage while still being practical.

I've collected old metal hose reels of various designs that I find interesting enough to have in the garden even without hoses on them. Using a garden hose of a neutral color—olive green or black—generally means your eye won't go to it first and linger there instead of on the plantings or other attractive focal points in the garden. Thank you, Martha Stewart, for those affordable gray-green garden hoses.

BOXES, BIRDHOUSES, AND OTHER PARAPHERNALIA

Birdbaths, birdhouses, doghouses, playhouses, swing sets, jungle gyms, sandboxes, electrical boxes, cable boxes—this list of things that provide services to a house or serve some function in a home landscape could go on. All can function well or poorly and all can add to or detract from the overall beauty of a garden, depending on their siting and treatment. Given the specific examples already discussed, I hope you can now contemplate these and determine ways to derive or create beauty from their function.

The same principle of developing beauty from function can successfully be applied to amenities other than the ones discussed so far that are necessary in landscapes

Even cellar doors can add beauty and interest to a garden. Here at Silas Monsieur's garden in Nutley, New Jersey, the doors display leaf imprints as a work of art.

A hose reel also functions as a work of art in Silas Monsieur's garden in Nutley, New Jersey.

With this architectural treatment, a pumping station in the University of Minnesota Arboretum doesn't mar the scene.

A utility powerhouse in The Rocks, a park in Washington, D.C., is disguised as a quaint outbuilding.

serving the public, even though the scale of such landscapes is generally much larger than residential gardens. If this principle were followed more frequently in the development of public landscapes, perhaps home gardeners would learn from them and follow their example.

PARKING LOTS

Parking lots are to public properties as driveways are to residential ones. Frequently they make the first impression, but usually they're treated with little thought of the visitor's experience (although savvy marketers are starting to realize the advantages of recognizing the parking lot as part of the total package). We experience examples of harsh and arid expanses of asphalt daily, but there are also examples to praise. At Superstition Springs Center, a large shopping mall in Mesa, Arizona, landscape architect Christie Ten Eyck created a landscape celebrating the sense of place in the parking lot and making a visit pleasurable from the moment a person arrives. The pedestrian walkway that leads shoppers through the parking lot to the mall is more akin to a nature trail than a sidewalk. The winding walkway of fine gravel is lined on both sides by berms displaying a rich selection of Arizona native plants, labeled as if in a botanic garden.

At Longwood Gardens in Kennett Square, Pennsylvania, a several-hundred-car parking lot also makes a welcoming entrance since a shaded walkway through the middle of the lot naturally attracts and guides visitors to the visitor's center. Trees planted along the meandering walkway are underplanted with a tapestry of ground covers and shrubs, creating the first display garden before visitors even reach the admission booth. The use of many broad-leaved evergreens and hedges on the outer edges of the planting beds that outline the walkway means that cars are largely blocked from view, just as in the Superstition Springs Center example. Even during the dormant period, when many visitors still come to Longwood to

The pedestrian walkway at Superstition Springs Center in Mesa, Arizona, creates a sense of place and welcomes shoppers.

enjoy inside conservatory displays, the entrance walkway makes the parking lot experience pleasant.

The Brandywine Conservancy in Chadds Ford, Pennsylvania, aims to preserve not only the artwork of the Wyeth family, largely displayed inside the Brandywine River Museum, but also the picturesque Pennsylvania countryside that inspired these artists. At the museum, most of the outdoor native plant garden is in the parking lot. Asphalt and gravel expanses are punctuated by broad raised planting bands full of native plants such as phlox, black-eyed Susan, Joe Pye weed, aster, and goldenrod, as well as naturalized species indicative of Pennsylvania such as daylilies and Queen Anne's lace. One of the parking lot gardens even contains a small pond. There yellow flag iris, bald cypress, winterberry holly, and other such water-loving natives capture the essential feel of wet areas found in the region. Only when you learn that the pond is really the storm water retention basin do you realize its important function, since it appears as a beautiful wetland garden.

STORM WATER

The Brandywine River Museum aside, public and commercial sites often end up handling storm water—another increasingly important demand—in a manner that results in what looks like an abandoned mud pit, but there are examples to demonstrate that even that challenge can be met in a way that creates beauty.

At Temple University's Ambler, Pennsylvania, campus, where horticulture and landscape design courses are taught, the faculty and students designed and built a

At Temple University's Ambler campus, storm water from a gutter becomes the inspiration for a wetland garden.

The creative handling of storm water at the Scott Arboretum in Swarthmore, Pennsylvania, led to the development of a "biostream."

A pump incorporated into this former garden of mine makes the cinder-block catch basin for storm water look attractive. The water that puddles there in the wet season makes the pump look realistic even though there's no well.

garden based on rainwater and storm water runoff. Gutters from several buildings empty into an overhead series of cascading wooden channels, like small aqueducts, carrying the runoff to a garden area where the water spills out the end into a central water feature composed of tile-mosaic-covered columns. From there it's allowed to flow into a wetland, a groundwater recharge area. Walkers can experience a distinct garden of bog plants and wetland plants from a boardwalk.

At the Scott Arboretum of Swarthmore College, what would have been a storm water drain and underground pipe became an abstraction of a natural stream. Storm water is allowed to flow for about fifty yards through an open channel lined with landscape fabric covered with river rock before tying back into the underground storm water pipe system. Runoff is thus allowed to percolate into the ground as it passes through this channel. Planting its banks with yellow flag iris, obedient plant, Joe Pye weed, Virginia sweetspire (*Itea virginica*), and other native or naturalized plants that thrive in wetlands or by streams has imbued the "biostream" with gardenesque qualities.

These examples of handling storm water or rainwater are applicable to home landscapes as well. In a previous Pennsylvania garden of mine, the gutters of the house fed underground to an open cinder-block box away from the house on lower ground, where the storm water was discharged unattractively. I put a lid of flagstone on the box, added an old hand water pump that looked convincingly antique, and planted Japanese iris in the wet ground around it to make the box look like a wellhead.

Jeff Jabco and Joe Henderson took that concept a step farther and dug a pond in their garden to be fed by the rain collected in the gutters of their house in Swarthmore, Pennsylvania. The captured rainwater allows them to grow lotus, and their runoff water doesn't add to storm water loads on the local creeks. Such "rain gardens" give the opportunity to grow different plants, but more important, they have a tremendous positive effect on groundwater recharge and the quality of streams, and they help ease the problems of erosion and flooding.

DRINKING FOUNTAINS

Another kind of water—drinking water—needs to be provided for visitors at public sites. This need, too, can give rise to beautiful and imaginative gardenworthy features.

At Chanticleer in Wayne, Pennsylvania, a drinking fountain for visitors becomes a water feature when in use. Excess from the jet of water drains out of a copper bowl through a wooden spout and spills onto a flat stone on the ground cut into the shape of a giant leaf with prominent veins. The veins then become darker channels as the water flows through them and off the edge of the leaf, into the garden beds where it then waters the plants growing there.

In a naturalistic rock garden at the New York Botanical Garden, a simple fountain that could be used for drinking or cooling one's hands takes on the

When visitors drink from a fountain at Chanticleer, the excess water flows into the carved stone leaf on the ground and out into the garden through its recessed veins.

A water fountain in the rock garden of the New York Botanical Garden in the Bronx.

A drinking fountain that doubles as a sculptural water feature at the Karl Dalberg School in Germany.

A drinking fountain that blends gracefully with its surroundings in Portland's Japanese Garden.

personality of a tapped spring along the trails of the Smoky Mountains. A small pipe at right angles to a wooden post shoots water out into a log trough. From there the overflow spills through a notch at one end of the log and flows into a streamlet that runs through the garden.

In other gardens I've seen drinking fountains appear as stone sculpture, with the spent water flowing over the outside of the stone to accent the colors of it. At the Van Dusen Gardens in Vancouver, British Columbia, a green stone cut into a crystalline form offers a simple jet of drinking water. The water flows over the stone, creating a beautiful glistening surface.

At the Japanese Garden in Portland, Oregon, a copper drinking fountain basin set on top of a boulder is shaded by a Japanese maple and hugged by a camellia and azaleas. With this treatment, the fixture does nothing to jeopardize the beauty and spirit of the garden while still conveniently and obviously providing drinking water.

BOLLARDS

Bollards, used in many public landscapes to keep cars off walkways, are typically some type of metal post that folds down or can be lifted out to allow service vehicles to enter as needed. Indeed, these are necessary evils in the landscape, but at the Brandywine River Museum, authentic old hitching posts are used as bollards to keep cars from galloping across the main entrance walkway. Such posts can be slipped into a pipe sleeve at their base so they can be removed readily when need be.

At the Sonoran Desert Museum outside Tucson, Arizona, large blue rocks of azurite function as bollards to protect a space for pedestrians gathering at the entry plaza. While separating pedestrians from vehicular traffic, these rocks from mines in Arizona begin to educate visitors about unique aspects of Arizona, which is the mission of the institution, as soon as the visitors get out of their cars. Bollards can contain and control traffic and still add to the sense of place and beauty, as they do in these examples.

BIKE RACKS

Bike racks can certainly blemish a site if the landscape design doesn't take them into account or if a need for them isn't recognized as part of the overall design. In the historic part of the University of Delaware campus, black pipes with caps and large, sturdy rings through their tops, to which chains or locks can be fastened, resemble old-fashioned hitching posts in front of the red brick colonial-style buildings. Their character is sympathetic with the wrought iron hardware on the buildings and the black metal light fixtures on campus. In this instance,

At the University of Delaware in Newark, Delaware, newly made posts serving as bike hitches take inspiration from old horse hitching posts.

This bike rack area at the College of the Atlantic in Bar Harbor, Maine, was designed to complement the materials used in buildings on campus.

In yet another example from a campus setting, this bike rack at the University of Minnesota Arboretum derives beauty from function.

when bikes are absent, the bike racks don't take away from the elegance of the university's central green area, the most visited and photographed section of the campus. On the campus of the College of the Atlantic in Bar Harbor, Maine, simple wooden posts—probably four-by-fours—are set vertically in a gravel bed edged with cobblestones, making a neat bicycle area that uses materials compatible with the rustic shingle style of the buildings on campus.

At parks I've seen fallen trees converted to bike stands by notching them every few feet. Not only is this a way to use fallen trees, but it also fulfills a need without inserting something obviously man-made that would visually conflict with the beauty of such natural areas.

LIGHTS AND TRASH CANS

Outdoor lights and trash cans—common in public landscapes—both play critical roles, and the style of these fixtures and their siting are key to either complementing or detracting from the beauty of the site. Safety in the case of lights and access in the case of trash cans may in part restrict or dictate the siting of these fixtures, but they needn't become unworthy focal points.

Fixtures need to be chosen with consideration of the architectural style of the site they will partner with. Modern light fixtures may jar the look of historical buildings, while Victorian reproduction fixtures, though beautifully ornate, may wind up looking trite on simple modern buildings. At the Brandywine River Museum, the light fixtures are made of exposed wooden boards. Now weathered, they have a hue that blends with the wooden shutters, shingles, and siding on the old brick mill, now the museum. These light posts also double as trellises for such natives as trumpet vine (*Campsis radicans*). Thus at the same time as the light fixtures illuminate the parking lot, they also blend pleasingly into the garden and provide a means for native vines to become part of the plant display.

DEER PROTECTION

In both residential and commercial settings in much of the country, protecting plants from deer has become a vexing problem for many, and providing this protection while not detracting from the aesthetics is indeed a challenge. Spicy sprays on plants may make the foliage unpalatable to deer, but they require continual and well-timed treatments and are expensive due to the labor involved. So while creating barriers or adding fencing isn't the only way to approach this problem, it frequently becomes the practical solution. Many public gardens have spent hundreds of thousands of dollars fencing their properties with the most basic fences, which don't lend a lot of beauty. The cost of a fence that functions well—that's tall enough to keep deer out—can be dauntingly high for homeowners as well, never mind trying also to make it visually pleasing and unimposing.

At the Morris Arboretum, a colorful structure protects the trunk of this young tree from buck rub while also adding a sense of whimsy to the garden.

David Benner, who has a fine woodland garden full of choice native wildflowers near deer-infested New Hope, Pennsylvania, developed an economical and effective method for deer exclusion that doesn't detract from the garden's beauty. He strings black plastic mesh fencing between trees to maintain his borrowed views into the woodland surrounding his garden. The mesh essentially disappears in the landscape, blending with the colors of the woods. His system was so sought after by other frustrated gardeners that he developed a horticultural business offering this form of deer protection. Perhaps this approach offers a corollary to the principle of developing beauty from function: if what you need can't be developed in a way to add beauty, at least approach it so it doesn't take away from the beauty.

In addition to needing protection to prevent deer browse, young trees are particularly susceptible to buck rub, when the males rub the velvet off their new antlers onto the trunks. Caging trees with unattractive rings or boxes of wire is a common response; however, the Morris Arboretum in Chestnut Hill, Pennsylvania, demonstrated the possibility of having fun with the solution by creating various artistic devices to provide such protection. Forms surrounding the trunks resemble giant skeletons of lampshades or lanterns; some are even painted in bright colors to accentuate the forms.

The need to protect street trees in urban settings from being banged up by car doors is similar to the need to protect trunks in rural or suburban settings from buck rub. Attractive metal guards to protect the trunks as well as plates to protect the root zones of street trees are now relatively standard in urban plantings.

WHERE TO FIND DESIGN INSPIRATION FOR APPLYING THIS PRINCIPLE

Since agriculture played a large role in the development of American culture, we can look to patterns and antecedents from rural and farming landscapes to provide inspiration for applying the principle of developing beauty from function. Coastal communities where fishing was the traditional basis for people's livelihoods and areas in the West where mining took place also have distinct architectural forms and layouts based on those activities, and these antecedents may provide an appropriate source of design inspiration.

At the heart of every farm is a barn, which, at least if it's not the metal prefabricated version, can offer beauty and provide inspiration for design. In some ways early barns, with their hand-hewn timber frames, have a simplicity of construction and a palette of materials similar to a Japanese teahouse. So why not look to the barn when trying to design a house, a picturesque garden structure, or a guesthouse in agricultural settings? Each part of the country has its own unique form and style of barn, just like fences. Barns in Pennsylvania may have Amish hex signs decorating them; those in Kentucky typically have vented sides to allow for the drying of tobacco; those in Maine tended to be attached to the house with a connecting room or passageway.

Weathervanes, generally placed on top of barns, once provided essential information to farmers. Today www.weather.com has perhaps made their role obsolete, but as ornaments in the garden or on a building, their appeal as examples of early American folk art is evident in the numerous reproductions available today. Whale weathervanes belong near the sea and bucking broncos in the "Wild West" to avoid a sense of geographical confusion.

In Europe, cattle feeding troughs of antique stone are prized as garden containers, especially for alpine plants. While stone troughs weren't common in America's

The beauty of farmland and fields inspired the creation of this garden at Chanticleer in Wayne, Pennsylvania. Some years it's an ornamental wheat field; other years, corn or millet is grown.

An agricultural practice has become an artistic expression in the garden known as Naumkeag in Stockbridge, Massachusetts, where the pattern of trees in an orchard and the unique forms of trees resulting from pruning are seen.

Barns, an icon of the American farm landscape, show distinct regional differences. Red barns are common in Wisconsin. This one is Neil Diboll's in Westfield, Wisconsin.

Traditional barns have just as much beauty as Japanese teahouses but have a cultural link to our landscapes. Here at Old World Wisconsin in Eagle, Wisconsin, a preserved barn shows a Finnish influence.

A new garden structure at Montrose in Hillsborough, North Carolina, clearly draws inspiration from the corncrib.

A garden toolshed displayed at AmeriFlora '92 in Columbus, Ohio, also borrowed its look from the corncrib.

Weathervanes capture a sense of place at the Albuquerque Biological Park in New Mexico.

A galvanized steel cattle watering trough has been turned into a small lotus pond.

At Old World Wisconsin, water pumps preserved in the farm/outdoor museum are displayed as an integral element in the agricultural landscape.

Another example of a water pump at Old World Wisconsin clearly shows its agricultural ties.

agricultural past, corrugated steel livestock watering troughs and wooden feed troughs convert into handsome ornamental water features or planters while retaining ties to farming traditions.

Hand pumps, used to extract water from subterranean wells, clearly provided a critical function for early settlers. Though for the most part these pumps have now been replaced with electric pumps for those still living in areas without city water, many original outside wells and their related pumps still remain in rural landscapes. Different parts of the country display wells and pumps with distinct regional styles, just like different parts of the country exhibit distinct forms of fences. Like the Japanese stone lantern, pumps may be obsolete today, but their form and ties to history may serve as inspiration for an ornamental garden feature that fits with our heritage. We might also borrow from our history of wells and hand pumps to meet our continuing need for garden spigots that lend beauty and interest to the garden.

Farm animals as "living garden sculpture" may bring more beauty and joy into a garden or landscape than expensive art or sculpture could contribute. Bantam chickens pecking through your garden add color and animation, and may even help control insect pests. David Culp in his Pennsylvania farmhouse-garden has bantams that roost in a quaint and attractive chicken coop. The coop, in a prominent spot in his garden, works as an architectural focal point.

A simple garden water spigot becomes a charming water feature due to its treatment at Mount Cuba Center in Greenville, Delaware.

At the Dawes Arboretum in Newark, Ohio, an original water pump still adds charm to the landscape.

A water pump accents a small town garden where the artist Charles Demouth once lived in Lancaster, Pennsylvania.

In Albuquerque, New Mexico, a simple water spigot adds utility and charm to this courtyard.

Those who raise Belted Galloways clearly do so out of appreciation for the picturesque quality of this antique cattle breed, but I've known gardeners to plan their garden layout or landscape views to take advantage of the sight of black sheep, or through to a pasture where horses graze. Frank Cabot in his garden near Quebec trained his Highland bull with his massive horns to frequent a spot visible at the end of a long formal garden vista by rewarding him with treats at the time of day he and his guests would likely be on the garden terrace relaxing and looking in that direction.

Don Shadow, renowned nurseryman of Shadow Nurseries, located near Winchester, Tennessee, has pastures for traditional farm livestock such as donkeys and exotic breeds such as ostriches (and many other rare and endangered animals) as an integral part of his nursery. Picture windows in his nursery office take advantage of such views.

At the Morris Arboretum in Chestnut Hill, Pennsylvania, black sheep graze on a green pastoral hillside beside the entry road as it winds up a hill following the contours of the land like a meandering farm lane. The sheep are a strong visual symbol of the former agricultural character of the land even though today the arboretum is surrounded by suburban development. After the initial glance, visitors may realize that they're two-dimensional sheep made of steel plates, but they create a peaceful rural mood in a convincing manner without the chores and expense of caring for livestock.

Similarly, borrowing from orchard landscapes where bee boxes would be brought in to help pollinate the fruit trees, Richard Bitner added bee boxes to his rural garden, I think originally more for their architectural interest than for the

A sculptural cow on a California property appears as though it could be grazing.

Two-dimensional sheep help create a rural mood at the entrance to the Morris Arboretum in Chestnut Hill, Pennsylvania, an area where housing developments have now replaced most of the farms.

A functioning chicken coop in David Culp's garden in Downingtown, Pennsylvania, looks like a small barn.

Permanent birds perched on the rocks give a sense of life to the landscape at Sol y Sombra in Santa Fe, New Mexico.

A scarecrow on public display at Longwood Gardens in Kennett Square, Pennsylvania.

The scarecrow at Stone Crop in Cold Spring, New York, said to be Gertrude Jekyll in effigy, suggests that we're still under the influence of British gardening.

Bee boxes provide not only honey but also an interesting focal point in Richard Bitner's Rheinhold, Pennsylvania, garden.

A scarecrow as a work of art in the garden of Ed and Amy Borer in West Chester, Pennsylvania.

promise of honey. Soon after realizing his bees weren't partial to white boxes, he painted them lavender, playing off the garden colors. The honey is a bonus.

From American farming traditions we have our own distinct forms of scarecrows, which are very different in appearance from the Japanese scarecrow described earlier. Adding a scarecrow to your garden can be an inexpensive way of adding sculpture even if you don't have crows to worry about.

Turning to antecedents from mining and returning to Superstition Springs Center in Mesa, Arizona, as an example, the dramatic water feature at the center of that landscape (pictured in the last chapter of this book) drew its form from the mining sluices found in the intermountain region. Similarly, recall how the industrial ruins at the Hagley Museum (described in the first chapter) determined the direction and development of the garden architecture and style there.

GENERAL GUIDELINES TO KEEP IN MIND
WHEN APPLYING THIS PRINCIPLE

To successfully apply the principle of deriving beauty from function, consider these corollaries. The original function or purpose of the object must be honored in some way; otherwise it looks useless and then regardless of how inherently beautiful the artifact is, it fails on some level. This means, for instance, that benches must be level. It doesn't feel right to sit on a bench that causes you to lean, so a bench doesn't look right if it's set at an angle, even if you never sit on it. It means that stepping-stones must be placed solidly so they don't teeter and totter underfoot, throwing you off the path rather than keeping you on track. It means that if you're going to add a well (or the suggestion of one), you shouldn't plant your water bucket full of posies. Similarly, don't put your sundial in the shade of a tree. This also means you should skip the floating section of fence (unless it functions as a horse jump). Like the "shutters" stapled onto subdivision homes, short free-floating sections of fence have lost their integrity. And put your two-dimensional Holsteins and merino sheep out in the pasture—not at your doorstep—if you want them to work. Livestock has always been separated from the formal entrance of the manor house or farmhouse.

Miniaturization will also get you into trouble, so don't do it. Leave the miniature wishing wells and windmills to the putt-putt golf courses. Windmills are picturesque icons in the rural landscape, but seeing a five-foot windmill in the front yard of a suburban house does little to conjure up the beauty or function of the real McCoy, which is the problem with the minibarns for storing mowers. Preserving the authentic scale is one way of honoring the original function of the structure, whether windmill, wishing well, or barn. Rescue and preserve a real windmill, and it will make a striking garden addition whether or not its power draws water.

And don't be artistic just for the sake of being artistic. The S-shaped front walkway laid out on a flat bare lawn comes to mind as an example. Unnecessary or arbitrary curves in walkways don't add beauty, they just make it annoyingly hard to stay on the path when you're trying to reach the front door or other destination. If there's no obvious reason to curve the path, it feels silly to follow such curves when a straight line would get you there more efficiently. If you want to slow visitors down on a garden path, you can effectively employ curves to do that, but plant trees or shrubs or create a rock outcropping in the way of the path so that it *has* to take a bend, so that it has a reason to be longer and meander.

If you can't afford the real functioning thing, take a pass on it and instead spend your money on something of genuine quality or integrity.

3

Use Humble Materials

GARDENS SHOULD GIVE US a sense of comfort, a sense of pleasure and gratification. They shouldn't overwhelm or intimidate or cause anxiety. They should have more in common with the family room or den of a house than with the formal living room, where when I was growing up neither food nor drink were permitted for fear of spoiling the good sofa or staining the carpet. The activities of living didn't take place in the living room; instead, it was the family room that invited us in, that allowed us to have fun and freely participate in all kinds of activities. We were at home in that room because it fostered pleasure and intimacy. For a garden or home landscape to be as inviting as a family room, it needs to convey a mood of modesty and casualness, a feeling that you're welcome and are free to explore, discover, relax, or experience the space through social activity. Using materials familiar and tied to the land helps accomplish this mood, whether they're indigenous, natural, or recycled materials. So the third principle is: use modest or humble materials in making your garden if you want it to nourish your spirit.

The late, great garden writer Henry Mitchell served up this bit of garden-making advice as follows:

> Avoid any show of wealth. This is marvelously easy for many of us. Do not permit anything in the garden to be more costly, in material, than is necessary. If wood poles will serve, don't use brick columns. If brick will do, don't use stone. If stone will do, don't use marble. (*The Essential Earthman*, 1981, 71)

Harland Hand used humble materials to create a vision of nature in his hillside garden in Berkeley, California. The "boulders" and "stones" he artfully created from concrete were no doubt far more economical than the real boulders and stones he might have imported into the steep space.

VALUING *WABI-SABI*

To jump back to Japan where I learned this principle, in the most revered gardens, rarely does one observe materials obviously displaying wealth. There are no gilded carved statues, nor is there precious or semiprecious stone inlay. Instead, one encounters broken old roof tiles embedded in clay forming garden walls, old building foundation stones converted into washbasins, and old bridge piling stones reused to shore up the edges of garden ponds—all discarded or recycled items. When new materials are employed, they're typically left untreated or are treated so subtly that they blend in as an element of the garden or give the feeling that they originated in the garden. For example, freshly cut green bamboo culms are one of the most popular materials to build fences with in Japan, and cryptomeria logs, lightly charred to darken their tone and help repel insects, commonly serve as the support posts for the bamboo.

The Japanese terms *wabi* and *sabi*, for which there are no clear or direct translations, refer to simple elegance and patina from age, two characteristics respected and cultivated in Japanese gardens, traditional architecture, and much of the pottery and artwork associated with the Japanese tea ceremony. The concepts of *wabi* and *sabi* have been developing in Japan since the sixteenth century, and today the two words are combined in a much-quoted phrase referring to the Japanese discipline of combining *wabi*, things that are simple or humble, and *sabi*, things that gain beauty from age. This *wabi-sabi* characteristic is, I believe, one of the reasons that we come home from visiting Japanese gardens and long to create a Japanese feeling in our own gardens. It is the *wabi-sabi* character, not the Japanese cultural aspect, that affects us. We simply have not yet learned to distinguish between *wabi-sabi* and the cultural aspect.

Robyn Griggs Lawrence, in her book *The Wabi-Sabi House* (2004), further explains the terms this way:

> *Wabi* stems from the root *wa*, which refers to harmony, peace, tranquility, and balance. Generally speaking, *wabi* had the original meaning of sad, desolate, and lonely, but poetically it has come to mean simple, unmaterialistic, humble by choice, and in tune with nature. . . . *Sabi* by itself means "the bloom of time." It connotes natural progression—tarnish, hoariness, rust—the extinguished gloss of that which once sparkled. It's the understanding that beauty is fleeting. (19–21)

For further insight, consider Leonard Koren's proposal in his book *Wabi-Sabi for Artists, Designers, Poets and Philosphers* (1994) that for something to be *wabi-sabi*, it has to give the suggestion of natural process and be irregular, intimate, unpretentious, earthy, murky, and simple (62–71). He interprets the application of this concept to the garden or landscape thus:

At the Biological Park in Albuquerque, New Mexico, a ramada provides shade while speaking of desert plants and revealing their structure.

> *Wabi-sabi* represents the exact opposite of the Western ideal of great beauty as something monumental, spectacular, and enduring. *Wabi-sabi* is not found in nature at moments of bloom and lushness, but at moments of inception or subsiding. *Wabi-sabi* is not about gorgeous flowers, majestic trees, or bold landscapes. *Wabi-sabi* is about the minor and the hidden, the tentative and the ephemeral: things so subtle and evanescent they are invisible to vulgar eyes. (50)

The modest and humble materials of Japanese gardens (or Italian, French, or English) may lose their humbleness upon importation into American gardens. The very process of importing them turns them into exotic, unfamiliar, expensive, pretentious, special, and complicated artifacts. Here they impress us, they strike viewers as precious novelty items, treasures painstakingly selected and transported from abroad. Seeing a Japanese stone washbasin made from a recycled foundation stone in a garden here makes me wonder about the shipping bill and cost of installation rather than feel comfort, closeness, or a sense of intimacy from its patina. A corollary to this principle, then, is: use indigenous materials, materials close at hand or sympathetic to the flavor and history of the region, because that, in part, is what gives materials a modest, comfortable personality.

STICKS

Plain logs—whether of eastern red cedar (*Juniperus virginiana*), black locust (*Robinia pseudoacacia*), or osage orange (*Maclura pomifera*) in the eastern half of the country or western red cedar (*Thuja plicata*) or ponderosa pine (*Pinus ponderosa*) in western regions—should be to the American garden what bamboo and cryptomeria are to the Japanese garden. As Erik van Lennep of Stratford, Vermont, wrote to *Fine Gardening* magazine (September/October 1989), bemoaning the use of teak shipped from rain forests in Southeast Asia, "There are plenty of positive reasons to build and buy garden furniture made here, from local woods, by local people. . . . the satisfaction of being able to identify the seat in our gardens with a known and positive chain of local events gives more meaning to our relationships to our world."

Van Lennep's sentiments echo values articulated during the Arts and Crafts period in this country and draw from a philosophy developed by Gustav Stickley, although Stickley dealt primarily with interior decorative arts at the start of the twentieth century. He developed and disseminated the philosophy and design approach of the English Arts and Crafts movement to a national audience in the United States. While the movement originated with William Morris in Britain, here the movement developed a distinctly American personality; in fact, some consider Stickley's designs to be the first original American furniture. Stickley's philosophy encouraged homeowners to have nothing in their homes that was not beautiful, and the movement eschewed mass machine production and the nonfunctional ornamentation of the Victorian era in favor of the handmade and the functional. His simple, well-made, clean-lined furniture was created from the finest grained quarter-sawn white oak, much of which he inspected himself before allowing it to be used. White oak, itself a symbol of America, possessed strength, beauty, and durability—qualities Stickley promoted in shaping a new American aesthetic through the design of everything from houses to textiles, an aesthetic outlined in detail in his magazine, *The Craftsman*.

Van Lennep's sentiments are also recorded in a verse that dates from an even earlier era, when chestnuts were still a defining feature of our eastern landscapes. The unknown author of this traditional verse attests to the powerful and meaningful associations that can develop between a plant, a region, and humans: "Born in a chestnut crib / Rocked in a chestnut rocker / Ate sweet chestnuts sitting in a chestnut chair / Made posts and rails 'til the day I died / Buried in a chestnut coffin."

Sticks, logs, and lumber can be used as a building material for many things in our gardens beyond garden furniture and fences. Recall all the artifacts and amenities outlined in the previous chapter. Branches from trees on your own property can be used to make stakes for peas and perennials or tripods for vine support while drawing little attention to themselves. Eastern red cedar logs with bark intact make handsome rustic garden gazebos, posts, and supports for porches, and serve well to support dinner bells, birdhouses, light fixtures, and clotheslines. They also can create compost bins while gracefully blending with the trunks of

A fallen tree is reincarnated as a garden bench with a few chain saw cuts.

An artistic fence made of sticks and twigs uses local materials at Olana, once the home of Hudson River School artist Frederic Edwin Church and now a historic-house museum in the Hudson River Valley of New York.

living trees in the garden. The stumps of dead or removed trees lend themselves as pedestals for birdbaths or feeders or posts to which hammocks can be secured.

At the Scott Arboretum of Swarthmore College, a grove of metasequoias was removed to make way for a new building. These unusual conifers were milled into shingles in anticipation of their use to side a new arboretum building. It was a way of honoring this grove of special trees while at the same time creating a useful and attractive building material. This was in part prompted by the desire to have building projects LEED (Leadership in Energy and Environmental Design) certified—more about that later.

Stumps and trunks in situ may also provide unique opportunities to add sculptural elements to gardens. At the Morris Arboretum in Chestnut Hill, Pennsylvania, the massive stump of a beech was turned into a fitting piece of "chain saw art" known as "Green Man." Visitors climb into the remnants of the trunk—now sculpture—and look out through the eyes of the massive carved leafy mask, thus appreciating both the magnitude of the trunk and the form of the sculpture in a firsthand, up-close way. The leaf face fittingly captures the character of the place, a place devoted to a collection of trees and other plants.

Carlton Goff carved a figure of Pan from a dead tree in his Rhode Island garden, leaving the natural flare of the trunk emerging from the ground to about four feet high. Pan, the Greek god of the woods, fields, and flocks, sits atop the stump but at the same time is part of it. He seems at home in the garden in all seasons with his goat legs, horns, and ears on his human torso.

When a tree died and presented the opportunity of its tall, straight trunk, Anne Winn had a totem pole carved. Animals stacked one on top of the other look out over her Pennsylvania garden as a column of guardian sentinels.

Stumps of trees cleared from the land are typically regarded as a burdensome waste material. But these, too, can be turned into treasure. I've seen picturesque barriers made by stacking stumps together and allowing them to weather. As the soil washes away and the bark disintegrates, exposing the shape of the roots, a picturesque tangle of tree skeletons and trunks emerges and makes a barrier or boundary as effective as any fence or stone wall.

Wood salvaged from deceased trees can be used in a multitude of ways in the home landscape—for benches, siding, fences, posts, decks, steps, and shingles, to name a few. If left unpainted, the grain of the wood changes color and develops a patina that documents the passage of time, a *sabi* characteristic. The browns, grays, and silvery tones that develop seem all the more harmonious with nature when compared to plastic or painted surfaces, which persist essentially unchanging or don't age gracefully. Part of the appeal of log cabins and other structures made of logs, I believe, comes from being able to look at the structure and see the direct link to nature through the materials; log houses reveal how many trees were used as well as their individual size and shape. In a recent newspaper article describing a new line of rough-hewn log homes offered by Orvis, customers are quoted as saying, "A log home offers a sense of roots and steadfastness and reconnecting with the past and the frontier ancestors you probably never had," and "It sounds very

Simple sticks become tripods for vines to grow on eventually, but in the meantime they blend with the garden.

In my own garden, rather than cut a white-barked birch to the ground I kept the stump to create a pedestal for a water tray.

Segments of vines have been crafted into a garden arbor at Grounds for Sculpture in Hamilton, New Jersey.

Teaching by example that with imagination, free material can be made into unique, one-of-a-kind garden treasures, the Morris Arboretum turned a tree stump into a giant mask called "Green Man."

Carlton Goff carved this Pan from a tree stump to watch over his Rhode Island garden.

corny, but you feel more connected to the land when you live in a log home" (Carey 2005). While these models are anything but modest in size, they still hearken back to humble roots by using humble materials.

Whether thin twiggy branches, massive trunks, or excavated stumps, all parts of trees can become useful building materials or offer unique opportunities for making elements of your garden conform to the principle of using humble materials.

A dead tree became a personal totem pole in the Pennsylvania garden of Anne Winn.

Slab boards maintain and display the character of the tree from which they were milled, thus creating obvious connections between this building in rural New York and the garden that surrounds it.

Stumps piled up and allowed to develop a silvery weathered beauty over time mark a boundary and make an effective barricade. Why do we bury stumps in landfills when they could lend such beauty and function to landscapes?

STONES

Stones, like sticks, are also readily available in many parts of the country as an economical material. Stones often help define the character of the larger landscape and they speak of the natural history of the site if they're not imported from distant sources. Granite, serpentine, limestone, volcanic rock, marl, and glacial till all visually reveal the story of the landscape and thus help to create the sense of place.

Natural stones lend themselves to any number of uses, depending on their size and nature. River stones can be used to create an attractive edge to a natural stream running through a garden or convincingly create the sense of a stream, even where or when no water is present. They may transform a storm water drainage culvert into an attractive feature by creating the illusion of a stream, as was done at the Scott Arboretum with the biostream described in the previous chapter. Still larger natural stones may serve as stepping-stones, stairs, or rocks to sit upon, perch drinks upon, or simply rest your eyes upon.

Small, smooth river or beach stones rounded by tumbling in water have been used in gardens to form handsome mosaics. In the garden at Dumbarton Oaks, designed by Beatrix Ferrand, lies a notable work of stone art created by Italian stonemasons using thousands of river stones. In one garden room, a pebble mosaic

Rock harvested on the site, an abandoned bluestone quarry, became the main building material for the six-acre earthwork known as Opus 40 that was developed over the course of thirty-seven years by stone sculptor Harvey Fite in Saugerties, New York.

Stone in its natural state is used as sculpture in this Woodside, California, garden.

depicting a wheat sheath in shades of brown, tan, black, and white lies like a giant painting on the ground, submerged in a shallow pool of water to enhance the
colors of the stones. While this example is on a scale hard for modern homeowners to imagine duplicating, it reveals the intricacies and beauty that can be created
using just small natural stones. On the other side of the country at Lotusland in

Black river rocks create a striking contrast, in both color and texture, to the *Hakonechloa* planted in their midst.

Coarse river rocks placed next to the dainty foliage of *Raoulia australis* create drama at Amador Flower Farm near Sacramento, California.

Santa Barbara, California, small river stones in contrasting colors are also used in a decorative manner to create dramatic paving at the entrance to the formerly private residence. Something as simple as a line of river stones embedded in concrete paving can add contrast in texture and color and help tie the man-made to the natural world.

While stone unshaped by humans has the most direct tie to nature, quarried or manipulated stone is also a basic material made by the forces of nature; thus local stone in all forms is sympathetic to the garden and offers a "humble personality." Stone has traditionally been shaped into everything from the foundation stones of houses to the shingles on their roofs. Stone houses and houses with stone foundations seem to have emerged from the ground or garden when compared to houses of man-made material. While slate roofs are among the most expensive to install today, they still convey a "humble" personality because of their obvious connection to natural rock.

To preserve and honor the personality of stone, don't paint it, however you use it; otherwise, you'll mask a significant part of its humble nature and the visually harmonious link it makes to the broader landscape. My own home, a small bunga-

This stone mosaic graces the entrance to the residence at Lotusland in Santa Barbara, California.

Rock sculptured into a face seems like a natural part of the garden at Chanticleer in Wayne, Pennsylvania.

A boulder turned into a water feature still retains its natural shape. Small river stones form the bed the water drains through to be recirculated (Portola Valley, California).

This river rock chimney designed by Greene and Greene in Pasadena, California, seems to be as much a part of the garden as of the house.

Rounded river rocks were used to create columns in the Arts and Crafts style at a New York highway rest stop. Visitors are given the sense of an Adirondack camp with the materials of nature being so prominent in the building.

Rocks mixed with brick make this garden wall look as though it grew up out of the ground.

Rounded river rock making up this wall ties the property closely to the natural landscape of the Southwest.

With its earthy colors, slate used as a roofing material connects buildings visually and materially to the earth and the garden.

At some point, the stone walls and cedar shingles of the building that now serves as the headquarters of the Scott Arboretum were painted over. Removing the paint and replacing the shingles not only restored some of the original character of the building but also connected the edifice better with the garden.

low built in 1915, has a stone foundation giving way to stucco walls. The stone on three sides of the house is visible for one to three feet above the ground. On the fourth side, the hill drops away and exposes a full story of stone. The same stone used for the foundation was used for the front porch pillars. With stone anchoring the house in this way, it feels connected to the land and created from it; friends comment that the small house "sits lightly on the land." I'm only sorry that a previous owner painted the stucco white, thereby visually disconnecting the sand and the tiny pebbles making up the rough stucco from the earth tones of the stone foundation and the garden itself. I'm sure their intention was to "brighten the place up," but by doing so they lost a direct visual connection to natural materials and part of its genuineness, subtlety, and *wabi-sabi* character.

When the house that serves as the office building of the Scott Arboretum was renovated, a sense of connection between the house and the garden was regained by removing yellow paint from the gray stone foundation and from a section of stone wall by the front door. The building now seems to flow into the garden because the same locally quarried stone, Pennsylvania schist, was used to create various garden walls around the building.

EARTH

The earth itself is perhaps the ultimate humble material. Adobe, made by mixing mud and straw and forming it into blocks to be baked by the sun, is surely one of the oldest building materials in this country. Southwestern pueblos such as Taos and Acoma, New Mexico, claim to be the oldest continually inhabited dwellings

There's perhaps no humbler material than the earth itself. Walls and dwellings built from adobe bricks connect to the landscape in a profound way.

Dwellings at Acoma Pueblo, one of the oldest continually inhabited structures in the country, are made of adobe.

in the county, and they're made largely of adobe. Houses and walls or enclosures of adobe are shaped from the earth around them, so they're connected to the land in color and material. Without care and maintenance, they're eroded by wind and water and melt back into the land, leaving little trace. Now newly built houses in the Southwest are capitalizing more and more on the distinct look and character of adobe; using earth-toned paints and emulating the smooth walls of adobe and the flat roofs of traditional dwellings, they blend with historical structures even when they're not actually made of adobe.

Houses made of straw—straw-bale houses—could perhaps be regarded as modern descendants of the sod houses that settlers once constructed on the treeless western plains. Straw-bale construction is currently being promoted as a way to provide low-cost and energy-efficient housing, but this material with its humble origins is another example of using local regional materials that lead to regionally distinct forms.

PLANTS

While the native plant movement in this country has a basis in ecology and conservation, one of the reasons for the increasing popularity of native plants, I believe, is a desire to create landscapes expressive of the place in which they reside. Relying on native plants or naturalized plants that symbolize a region—the plants close at hand, like the sticks and stones—is also an expression of this principle. Some native plant promoters claim that native plants are better adapted to their home grounds than imported exotics, and that's the reason they should be relied upon. But that argument is a broad generalization not always holding true. When you consider how easily exotics such as kudzu, Japanese honeysuckle, and multiflora rose have settled into our landscapes, the half-truth is all too clear. Gardening with and growing native plants is generally just as much work and takes just as much effort as gardening with exotics, but native plants help preserve or create a sense of place in the same way as culturally based architecture does.

Using native plants can help to create a familiar picture and therefore a comfortable and inviting space. To my sensibilities, a great feeling of disconnection (of "geographical confusion" in Gertrude Jekyll's words) results when a property has been created by carving out a space from, say, the surrounding majestic eastern deciduous forest, and the house sits on a rectangular patch of lawn devoid of trees as though separated and protected by a green moat. The disconnect is particularly severe if the house is then surrounded by plantings of tight dwarf conifers and bright annuals, furthering distancing it from the visual and physical characteristics of the woods around it. The beautiful natural woods are no longer borrow-able because there's no sense of connection to them. Or in the Southwest, the same feeling of disconnection is created when a house is set on a patch of lawn amidst picturesque cholla or architectural ocotillo or palo verde. It's as though a placemat of lawn has been laid out and the house has been set upon it like a plate.

The saguaro cactus of Arizona, the redwoods of California, the pitcher plants of Georgia's savannas, the canoe birch of New England, the quaking aspen of Utah—these are examples of plants and regions of our country inextricably linked together. The plants have become powerful symbols of those places. That's the profound reason they should be used in landscapes and gardens, so Colorado continues to look like Colorado and Virginia continues to amaze us with its trilliums and Texas with its sweeps of bluebonnets. This was one of the key messages promoted by Lady Byrd Johnson and led to her establishing the Lady Byrd Johnson Wildflower Center in Austin, Texas. Highway departments around the country well beyond Texas are at last taking note, and native species are being used to landscape roadsides today. Thankfully, no longer do we find daylilies homogenizing the American landscape in roadside plantings from sea to shining sea.

On a more local level, individual species may epitomize and speak of different habitats. In the mid-Atlantic area, Joe Pye weed and American sycamores—because of their strong penchant to grow along waterways—represent stream valleys

The native Texas paintbrush (*Castilleja indivisa*) and bluebonnets (*Lupinus* spp.) make the Texas Hill Country spectacular in springtime.

or floodplains, while the evergreen Christmas fern occurs in the wild on north-facing slopes where its leathery leaves are typically shaded throughout the winter months when the sun is low in the sky. Having an understanding, a familiarity, with these associations of plants with place means that as a garden or landscape creator, you can use this knowledge to create strong and distinct moods and evoke emotions. Developing this kind of sensitivity will allow you to compose pictures that look right and don't create feelings of isolation or severed connections. Creating a garden that belongs to its place is a compelling reason to garden with native plants, although a planting exclusively of natives or a garden full of indigenous plants won't always be guaranteed to look at home and fit with its surroundings (but you learned about that in the first chapter).

RECYCLED MATERIALS

Making something out of sticks, stones, plants, and other materials native to a region represents the concept of using humble materials. Another way to create a powerful sense of modesty and humility is to make something for the garden from discards—essentially trash. All the landscape and garden amenities mentioned in the second chapter as opportunities to add beauty and function can be created from recycled materials. Let me outline some examples of successful and creative recycling in gardens I've admired.

Clamshells, cobblestones, and concrete

A friend of mine recalled how residents of his hometown of Muscatine, Iowa, used fragments of shell buttons to make paths and driveways. The shells of freshwater oysters harvested from the Mississippi River were the button factory's raw material; the fragments of buttons that were turned into pathway gravel were discarded from the factory as imperfect, a waste material.

Similarly, up and down the East Coast, in ports where clams have traditionally been harvested, crushed clamshells were used as a paving material, again as waste material from the clamming operations. (Laws now prohibit this, except for use at historical sites such as Colonial Williamsburg, and now the shells are returned to the ocean.)

In Philadelphia, a major seaport for the country in its early days, old city streets are paved with cobblestones, the discarded ballast from the early seafaring ships. Today many gardeners in the region recognize the beauty of cobblestones as a paving material, although they're no longer available dockside as discarded ballast. Cobblestones salvaged from repaired or repaved streets are being recycled yet again and cobblestones are also being freshly quarried and produced due to the popularity and demand for the old stones.

Slate and ceramic shingles removed from the roofs of barns, houses, and sheds have been used to create richly textured paths and garden sculpture. Garden makers have sunk them in the ground side by side so just the ends are exposed, making a richly textured, deep, and durable pathway. At Chanticleer in Wayne, Pennsylvania, a ruin garden was made from a demolished stone house. Salvaged roof tiles were embedded in flagstone to create a border around the floor in one of the open-air rooms of the ruin. The result resembles a carpet made of stone and recycled tile.

Clamshell fragments discarded by the fishing industry were traditionally used as a paving material in coastal towns, here in Edgartown on Martha's Vineyard.

Chunks of concrete have been diverted from landfills and reused to create pathways, patios, and walls, yielding surprisingly handsome results. Patios made of recycled concrete chunks have a beauty similar to those made of random-laid flagstones. Retaining walls of recycled concrete chunks reveal a rough, irregular surface, and steps formed from recycled concrete can make use of the flat smooth surface while exposing a textured surface of the stones used in the concrete mix on the face or riser of the steps.

Old tile roof shingles have been reused in the paving of the Ruin Garden at Chanticleer. Set end-up in flagstone, the tiles create a sense of an Oriental carpet in the open-air dining room, where the "table" is a water feature.

Old slates stacked and chipped make a rock urn in this small residential garden in Ludlow, England; the recycling of roof slates is an idea that also translates well across the Atlantic.

A corncrib has been converted into a picturesque footbridge across a seepage area draining into the lake at Innisfree, in Millbrook, New York.

Dilapidated buildings

Smokehouses, outhouses, and other abandoned or obsolete structures can be scavenged, saved, and converted into toolhouses, pavilions, or garden workshops, or used for garden tool storage. In the rural Pennsylvania garden of the late Joanna Reed, a round wire corncrib with a tin roof was added to the garden, where it became an inviting gazebo. No longer intended to store corn, it became both a focal point and a destination perched on a hillside, a place to sit and relax while viewing the garden below. Its personality was so in keeping with the farm character of the garden that visitors assumed it had always been on the property, when in fact her children gave it to her for her eightieth birthday, having acquired it from another farm.

In another example, a wooden, rectangular corncrib with sloping sides of lath was turned into a pedestrian covered bridge over a broad seepage area at Innisfree, an extraordinary garden in Millbrook, New York. Now open to the public, Innisfree was created as a stroll garden around a lake. The converted corncrib is one of the memorable places one discovers and passes through while journeying around the lake.

In his Pennsylvania farm garden, Richard Bitner converted the remnants of a stone springhouse into a garden pavilion. A quaint house was outlined by adding

Skeletons of buildings and structures can also be successfully recycled. Here a greenhouse skeleton was turned into a garden structure at Grounds for Sculpture in Hamilton, New Jersey. The vine-covered cast-iron remnants of a greenhouse now form a niche for a piece of sculpture.

The ruin of a springhouse has been turned into a garden pavilion in a Pennsylvania farm-garden by redefining its roofline.

An example of a barn recycled and converted into a residence in northern Delaware. As the largest "garden ornament," the barn-house complements a simple landscape that takes advantage of borrowed scenery, hedgerow trees, and humble materials such as the gravel used in the driveway.

a skeleton of a roof back onto the structure, but now the rafters support vines instead of shingles. The open-air building creates a magical place and an intimate room to discover in the garden.

At Grounds for Sculpture in Hamilton, New Jersey, a portion of an exhibition greenhouse remains from the days when the site hosted the state fair. Devoid of glass and flooring, the iron skeleton is intertwined with vines and now creates an arched foliage-covered alcove where one of the pieces of sculpture is attractively displayed. Using the ruins in this way gives visitors the opportunity to experience some of the 1930s architectural style and character of the former fairgrounds.

On a smaller scale, Saundra and Geoffrey Sheppard dismantled the skeleton of a residential conservatory from the turn-of-the-century and resurrected it in the garden of their new townhouse in Media, Pennsylvania. The open-air outline creates a distinct and intimate garden pavilion that conveys a sense of age and a by-gone era in the new garden. A metal table and chairs sit in the middle of the glass-less greenhouse and tropical plant baskets hang from the structure's cast-iron ribs during the growing season. From the ruins of a small glass house, the Sheppards have created an alfresco dining area in their garden far more memorable than any prefabricated gazebo.

In a residential garden in Media, Pennsylvania, a rescued greenhouse skeleton was reassembled to create an outside garden room.

Dan McNeal obtained an old railroad switching house measuring about ten feet by seven feet, an appropriate size for a garden toolshed, for his small urban garden in Downingtown, Pennsylvania. Its board-and-batten siding, overhanging eaves, and rural Gothic style complement his turn-of-the-century row house with similar rooflines and materials.

In nearly every town across the country, you can discover examples of school-houses, churches, factories, warehouses, train stations, and barns that have been adaptively converted into homes, shops, restaurants, and offices. All are expressions of the principle of using humble materials and can serve as inspiration.

Millstones, relics from America's early industrial past, have been recycled in numerous ways in gardens. At French Farm, David Wierdsma's garden in Greenwich, Connecticut, a massive millstone serves as a garden table that endures all kinds of weather with no special care.

Carlton Goff in his Rhode Island garden used a millstone as a pedestal for an armillary sphere (an astronomical instrument with rings marking important circles in the celestial sphere).

Millstones

Millstones are enduring artifacts from the early development of water-powered mills along rivers and streams up and down the East Coast. Superseded by electrical energy and modern machines, millstones have migrated into gardens, where they've been recycled into any number of features. In some cases they've simply been added as sculptural elements; in others they now serve a new function, as a threshold, a step, a seat, a table, or a fountain, but in all cases they provide a link to the past and remain beautiful artifacts. Now with the scarcity of authentic old ones, reproductions of millstones, like cobblestones, are even being made and offered in garden ornament catalogs.

A pair of millstones set on their edges and built into the ends of a wall create a memorable and regionally appropriate entrance to an estate in the Brandywine Valley. Henry Francis du Pont, creator of the garden at Winterthur in Greenville, Delaware, used millstones as threshold steps into antique garden gazebos and as pedestals for sculpture, thereby at least putting his imported English lead statues on a good Brandywine footing.

At a residential garden in Lancaster, Pennsylvania, a millstone has become a pleasing water feature.

A millstone is used simply as a planter at the historic Mohonk Mountain House in New Paltz, New York.

A millstone forms the heart of a deck at the Brandywine River Museum, Chadds Ford, Pennsylvania.

At the Brandywine River Museum in Chadds Ford, Pennsylvania, millstones have been used as paving stones, picturesquely punctuating the path that hugs the banks of the Brandywine River just outside the museum. The original museum building, which has had modern additions to it, was itself created from a former mill building. Other massive millstones have been used at points along the path as circular benches or platforms. In another application at this museum complex, a millstone forms the heart of a wooden deck. The boards of the deck were cut and laid in such a way as to visually extend the carved grooves in the millstone into the pattern of the larger deck surface.

In the garden of Yvonne England in Honeybrook, Pennsylvania, a water feature has been made from a millstone placed on top of a stone pedestal about three feet tall. A sheet of water flows over the surface of the millstone, drips off the edge, and falls into a small circular pool beneath. The recaptured water is pumped up from the pool through the pedestal and wells up through the center hole of the millstone. Yvonne outlined the details of making her millstone fountain in an article published in *Fine Gardening* (August 1995).

As mentioned earlier, in Japan old building foundation stones have been recycled into garden washbasins. The depression where a support post was once inserted serves well as a basin to hold a pool of water. The act of rinsing your hands at such a water basin to prepare for participation in the tea ceremony is all the more humbling given that this is a relic. Front door thresholds or steps or a water feature created from a millstone share that same kind of beauty, that same humble character. This, then, is a way to capture an American expression of *wabi-sabi* in the garden.

Yvonne England's millstone water feature is humble but effective.

A millstone in Brookgreen Gardens, a large public garden on the coast south of Myrtle Beach, South Carolina, makes a dramatic foreground for a flowering tree.

Millstones are set in paving at the Conestoga House and Gardens, open for public tours in the summer in Lancaster, Pennsylvania.

Recycled whiskey barrels have for years been popularly used in gardens as planters, fountains, and water features, for good reason. Their simple materials and patina mean they blend immediately with garden elements. In this example, a sculptural assemblage of sticks suggests that a heron is visiting the small half-whiskey-barrel pool.

A recycled whiskey barrel is grouped attractively with other planters at Wave Hill, a public garden and cultural center overlooking the Hudson River in the Bronx, New York.

Barrels and tubs

The aged oak whiskey barrels discarded from distilleries have long been popularly recycled in gardens and are very successful examples of practicing the principle of using humble materials. Cut into halves, they serve well as planters or small water gardens. Home gardeners with no more than a balcony can grow water lilies and lotus in a half-barrel that's affordable and easily manageable, and that has a personality harmonious with the colors of the garden.

Galvanized laundry tubs, wrought-iron cauldrons, and livestock watering troughs all have also been effectively converted into containers and water gardens, much like whiskey barrels.

Railroad ties have been recycled to create a bridge at a nursery in California.

Railroad ties

Like millstones, railroad ties have been given second lives in gardens after being re-moved from service. Steps, footbridges, pathways, decks, retaining walls, pedestals, posts, and bollards have all been created from recycled ties.

In William and Nancy Frederick's garden, Ashland Hollow, a mulched path leading up a steep hillside is stepped with recycled railroad ties. The edge of the garden where the shrub and perennial beds give way to meadow and buffer land is not unlike the wild edge of a train track. The brown ties blend well with the mulch and the meadow character of the hillside.

In Dan McNeal's small in-town garden, his recycled railroad-switching-house-become-toolshed is connected to the garden with steps and a deck made of old railroad ties that attach to his house. (A word of warning: true railroad ties have been treated with preservatives, which may make their use in certain situations inadvisable.)

Steps and a deck in a Downingtown, Pennsylvania, garden were made from recycled railroad ties.

Railroad ties are used as steps in a California residential garden.

Recycled granite city curbstones create a bridge at the Mount Cuba Center.

City curbstones are reused as the steps off of this terrace at Chanticleer, Wayne, Pennsylvania.

City curbstones and sidewalks

In older sections of some cities, curbstones of granite are being replaced with concrete curbing. In some cases the long, flat curbstones are salvaged and available for purchase. Contact your city's street department to learn if such stones are available, since these lend themselves to the making of beautiful garden features.

In the naturalistic pond garden created by Pamela Copeland near Greenville, Delaware, now a public garden known as the Mount Cuba Center, four city curbstones were used to create a bridge. Laid two abreast and connected by a keystone in the center of the bridge, they create a simple, small, but strong crossing over a spillway between two ponds. The character of the bridge is in keeping with the naturalistic wildflower garden.

In Media, Pennsylvania, recycled city curbstones were used to create steps through the hillside rock garden of Claire Muller, replete with craggy boulders. The curbstones-turned-steps blend with the beautiful naturalistic rockwork in the garden while providing level and easily navigable steps. One curbstone, still displaying the "no parking" yellow band painted on it during its city life, was appropriately used as the first step at the top of the hill where one begins the descent into the garden. Its yellow band now signals garden strollers to use caution.

At Chanticleer in Wayne, Pennsylvania, recycled city curbstones were laid end to end to create a series of wide, gentle steps leading off of a stone terrace. The terrace, backed by a fieldstone wall and with post-and-beam trelliswork overhead, resembles the remnants of an old bank barn, although it was created anew. The worn, rounded edges of the curbstones help to create the illusion more convincingly than could any fresh-cut granite steps.

The Borough of Swarthmore, Pennsylvania, kept its old stone curbstones and turned them into park benches simply by setting each old curbstone onto stone blocks to serve as legs.

In many towns, the city sidewalks themselves were originally made of large slabs of stone. These too are occasionally removed due to construction or to modernize. A Victorian estate in upstate New York that now serves as a public garden had such stone walkways throughout elaborate plantings. The staff became concerned that after a century, the surface of the stone in the walkways had been worn slick and smooth, so they had all the stone replaced with poured concrete. A local landscaper recycled the sidewalk stones into handsome residential patios that surely have the potential to last another century. Flipping the stones over assuaged worries about slipperiness. Sadly, the garden gave up a quiet natural material for bright light-reflective walkways that no longer have historical significance nor character in keeping with the property.

Other examples of creative recycling

There are countless examples of creative garden makers who have found the beauty, utility, and opportunity in recycled materials.

In a garden near Asheville, North Carolina, I marveled at a pergola constructed entirely of lath recovered when walls were demolished in a house renovation project. The structure had a unique textured appearance and the advantage of not appearing raw or new in the garden since the lath had already aged.

Bowling balls can frequently be found at yard sales for a song, and I've seen gardeners mix these into borders to add color and form in a playful way. Similarly, I've seen rusty barbed wire wound into balls and used as sculptural elements in gardens. Recycled remnants of farm equipment and machinery cost little to nothing and create evocative garden focal points that tell something of the past.

Old garden tools, broken or rusted beyond use, have been permanently parked in the garden as ornaments. In a small urban garden in Denver created by Susan Yetter, rakes with bent and rusty tines and with their handles stuck in the ground serve as vine supports. She also used an iron frame bed headboard to make another small-scale, attractive vine trellis.

Shards of broken pottery and ceramic dishes mixed into the gravel of pathways in Marcia Donahue's garden in Berkeley, California, add bits of color and history. As you look down and pick out the details in the gravel mix of her paths, you can spot bits of plates, saucers, and cups, not unlike spotting shells on a beach. Traveling the intimate paths soon feels like a treasure hunt.

Salvaged plywood was used to create this garden mural/wall/fence in the Village of the Arts in Philadelphia, Pennsylvania.

Lath salvaged from demolished house walls was recycled to create this garden structure.

Rusted wheels become objects of art at Amador Flower Farm in California.

A recycled remnant of a garden rake serves now as a vine support in a Denver garden.

An old grate becomes part of the garden path in this Lafayette, Indiana, garden.

Isaiah Zagar in Philadelphia, Pennsylvania, incorporates pottery and ceramic figures into celebrated outdoor mosaics. This gives a second life to objects broken during the process of importing them for Eyes Gallery, which he and his wife own on South Street. Whimsical bits of Mexican pottery from Oaxaca and Michoacán add rich detail to his garden artwork along with the mirrors and tiles he incorporates. The property at 1024 South Street is now known as Magic Garden, and a not-for-profit organization formed in 2004 to purchase the urban mosaic garden for posterity.

When I discussed this concept with a friend, she noted that she's seen a lot of junk recycled in gardens—painted tractor tires was the example that came to mind—which she finds lacking any satisfying artistic expression. There's a fine line, I suppose, between the artistic and creative recycling of found objects as garden art and the accumulation of junk. And as they say, "beauty is in the eye of the beholder." Having an artistic eye for composition, line, form, texture, balance, and color is critical to successfully incorporating discarded objects in the landscape, when those objects may not appear inherently beautiful to the average beholder.

ECOLOGY AND AESTHETICS

Using materials at hand and recycling items helps promote and preserve regional character, thereby creating a meaningful and pleasing aesthetic. Additionally, the principle of using humble materials has environmental benefits, and that aspect may be the force that helps the principle gain advocates and realize increased practice. Using local and indigenous materials has received a powerful boost from the U.S. Green Building Council, which has developed a set of criteria to guide and recognize environmentally sensitive building. Published in 2000, the Green Building Rating System sets standards in five broad areas for architects, builders, and project managers to consider during the design phase. Building projects earn credits for meeting these standards and are granted recognition and awards, based on the total number of credits garnered, for demonstrating Leadership in Energy and Environmental Design (LEED). There are Bronze, Silver, Gold, and Platinum LEED awards, which in turn lead to good publicity for the organization, whether profit or not-for-profit. The five areas in which credits can be earned are sustainable sites, water efficiency, energy and atmosphere, materials and resources, and indoor environmental quality. Many items outlined in the rating system relate to the landscape and the site, and many of these promote using local materials and recycling.

In addressing materials and resources, for example, the rating system document states that the intention is to "extend the life cycle of existing building stock, conserve resources, retain cultural resources, reduce waste, and reduce environmental impacts of new buildings as they relate to materials manufacturing and transport." Credits are awarded depending on the percentage of building materials obtained by recycling existing structures. Similarly, the section of the document on construction waste management states these intentions: "Divert construction demolition and land clearing debris from landfill disposal. Redirect recyclable material back to the manufacturing process." Here, credits are awarded based on the percentage by weight of waste materials that are recycled.

The LEED system also recognizes the value of local and regional materials. It states the following intention: "Increase demand for building products that are manufactured locally, reducing the environmental impacts resulting from transportation and supporting the local economy." Credit is awarded if a minimum of 20 percent of the building materials are manufactured within a radius of five hundred miles, and/or if a minimum of 50 percent of the building materials are extracted, harvested, or recovered within five hundred miles.

In summary, the LEED program is based on the environmental value of using local and recycled material in buildings and landscapes. Because of the ecological benefits and the public recognition granted, this program will in time help shape the aesthetics and the desired look of buildings. With the examples outlined in this chapter, I've argued that aesthetics don't have to be compromised to meet such ecological goals or standards and that aesthetics are, in fact, frequently enhanced with a sense of appropriateness stemming from such an approach.

As children we learned while playing in the garden that all kinds of things could be made from sticks, stones, cut grass, and mud—even pies. As adults making gardens, we need to relearn how to play with what we find in the garden and how to make humble materials into all kinds of wonderful and beautiful things for the garden and our enjoyment of it.

Marry the Inside to the Outside

VARIOUS RESEARCHERS have documented the therapeutic and health benefits of having a view to the outside. Patients heal faster in hospital rooms with windows looking out onto plants, gardens, or natural landscapes. In other studies conducted in low-income housing areas, those with even a minimal amount of landscaping had lower incidents of domestic crime and violence compared to those with no trees or landscaping (see Lewis 1996; Kuo and Sullivan 2001). Knowing that, it isn't much of a leap to assume that the more we can observe nature and have plants or gardens in our daily lives, the happier and healthier we'll be. And the more we connect our houses, schools, and offices to the outside, the more we'll be able to do that. The fourth principle, then, is to marry your house to your garden; blur the lines between the built and the natural, between the architecture and the landscape; bring the outside in and take the inside out.

If you visit many famous Japanese gardens, you soon learn that to see the garden, you must take your shoes off, don slippers, and enter a temple building. Only from the veranda or interior of the building is the garden revealed. Only by going inside can you fully experience the outside. Ryoan-ji, the world-famous rock garden on the outskirts of Kyoto, is an example of this. There, you sit on the veranda looking at the rock and gravel composition enclosed by an ancient wall made of mud, and you never actually step into the garden itself. Such gardens were designed to be viewed primarily from indoors, so a strong relationship clearly exists between the temple buildings—their form of architecture—and the garden. In fact, they're so integrated that one isn't complete without the other. We fall in love with such gardens in part because we've been able to observe them, to feel them, to connect to them. We do that because of the strong marriage between the inside and the outside.

THREE EXEMPLARY PROPERTIES

Some notable American properties exemplify this principle; I'll describe three here. One was designed by Frank Lloyd Wright; one was created by a celebrated industrial designer, Russel Wright; and the other was created by a lesser-known but accomplished artist-craftsman, Wharton Esherick. These properties, all now open to the public, are named or were once known for a natural feature found on the property, suggesting what the houses are connected to in their landscapes. They are, respectively, Fallingwater, Dragon Rock, and the Wharton Esherick Museum, dubbed "a Pennsylvania Hill House" at the 1940 World's Fair.

Frank Lloyd Wright, who was deeply influenced by visits to Japan and by Japanese aesthetics, excelled not only at having the site suggest the architecture but also at blending the inside to the outside. He demonstrated how to manifest the characteristics of the American landscape in the lines and forms of his houses, and he also employed strategies to incorporate elements of the houses' natural surroundings into the life inside. One of his most famous and celebrated houses, Fallingwater, built in 1936 outside Pittsburgh, Pennsylvania, is in a sense like a Japanese temple and its contemplative garden. You cannot fully experience the raw nature of Bear Run Creek and its waterfalls until you're inside the house. Perched above the waterfalls, the house has two massive cantilevered rectangular terraces, which you can step out onto from many rooms, including the living room. Thus the dramatic views of the stream and its valley available from the terraces are but a step or two away from the house's interior. A staircase descending to the water directly from the living room is another physical and symbolic linking of the house to the site and makes it possible to dangle your feet in the cold flowing water without needing to put on shoes or venture more than a few steps from the fireplace. And by siting the house as close to the falls as he did, Wright ensured that the sound of the water falling penetrates the interior spaces and is part of the experience of being in the house.

While the site focuses on the water, the rocks and plants of the surrounding landscape are also prevalent inside. Natural boulders exposed during the construction process poke up through the stone floor in the living room immediately in front of the fireplace, regarded by Wright as the heart of a house. Thus the bedrock the house depends upon is visibly exposed in its natural form. Indoor planting pockets literally bring the outdoors inside. Mountain laurel and mosses, seen growing outside, fill the pockets instead of exotic tropical houseplants. Abundant and unique windows also reveal views of the native vegetation. Most of the windows in the house aren't cloaked with curtains, and many windows turn corners

At Fallingwater, Frank Lloyd Wright's masterpiece, the inside is married to the outside in numerous ways. Here, the boulders the house is built upon can be seen penetrating the interior spaces.

with mitered glass so that a panoramic view to the outside isn't broken or interrupted by structural elements or window casings. The windows in a vertical three-story column open outward from the corner, making the edge of the building disappear while allowing the outside water-cooled air to come inside.

Viewed from the outside, the house seems to have grown from the site rather than having been imposed onto the site. The walls of the terraces, painted a cream color, are a striking feature of the house and mimic the white water of Bear Run Creek when the house is viewed from below the falls. By extending the sandstone forming the cliffs of the falls and the bed of the stream upward to form the walls of the house, Wright connected the materials and the appearance of the house to the site in yet another way.

The inside and the outside also merge between the main house and the guesthouse. Climbing the hill to the guesthouse, added in 1939, you pass through a wild landscape and look into rich woods at masses of rhododendron, mountain laurel, and dramatic rock outcroppings, while still having the protection of a ceiling since the walkway has a stepped canopy.

In summary, Fallingwater, considered a masterpiece and one of the best-known houses in the world, employs a variety of ways to capture a connection between the inside and the outside. Visitors profoundly feel the drama and beauty of the natural place because of the successful linking between the interior spaces and the natural beauty of the exterior spaces.

Dragon Rock, the house on the property known as Manitoga in Garrison, New York, is more modest but similar in spirit to Fallingwater. This house, designed by Russel Wright (no relation to Frank Lloyd Wright), is becoming increasingly celebrated, I believe, precisely because of how well it demonstrates the principle of marrying the inside to the outside. Russel Wright (1904–1976) was one of American's great industrial designers and introduced millions of Americans to modernism through his designs of dinnerware, furniture, appliances, and textiles. He and his wife, Mary, helped shape American society with their *Guide to Easier Living* published in 1950. After Mary died in 1952, Wright began designing a house and developing a landscape from an eighty-acre property they had purchased in 1942 that had been logged and had an abandoned quarry on it. The name of the house, Dragon Rock, came from their daughter, Ann; Manitoga refers to the surrounding landscape and means "place of the Great Spirit" in Algonquian.

Like Fallingwater, Dragon Rock holds hands with a dramatic landscape feature. It sits at the edge of the abandoned stone quarry, which Wright turned into a lake by channeling a stream into it. But that is not immediately apparent. To those who enter the property on the gravel driveway, as Wright would have done, the house is all but invisible, because it lies behind a grove of trees and a mound of boulders and clings to the rock face sloping down to the quarry. The roof of the house is only slightly higher than the grade of the entry drive. At first view, visitors are more apt to focus on the trees and the boulders than the house and may even wonder where the house is. The feeling is one of entering a beautiful natural area rather than arriving at a residence. Nor is the quarry-lake evident from the entry drive. Like Ryoan-ji's rocks, it is only revealed after one descends into the house. There, floor-to-ceiling windows and doors facing the lake dramatically reveal views and connect most of the rooms in the house to the lake and its surrounding landscape. (Here too, then, anyone performing the mundane rituals of daily life would take in views of a dynamic landscape feature, just as at Fallingwater with its marriage to Bear Run Falls.)

Stone, abundant on the former quarry site, was used to form terraces that make it easy to step outside directly from most rooms. And the stone continues across the thresholds, forming the floor in the dining and living areas, also similar to Fallingwater. Boulders, like those found along the woodland trails Wright used throughout the property, form a stairway rising from the garden-level dining room and winding up to the living room. Boulders also make up exterior and interior walls and rim the elevated interior living space overlooking the dining area. A massive tree trunk, complete with knots and furrows, forms the principal support column for the roof of the house, giving the impression that a tree grows through the center of the house. Native plants were replanted around the house immediately following its construction, thereby avoiding the feeling that a place for the house was carved out from nature.

At Dragon Rock, the house Russel Wright designed for himself in Garrison, New York, the rooms focus on the most dramatic landscape feature, an abandoned stone quarry he turned into a lake by diverting a stream.

Rocks form the floors and chimney of Dragon Rock, tying it directly to the rocks seen in this view of the quarry swimming hole.

Dragon Rock's use of large expanses of glass along with rock and logs inside the house ties the garden and house together.

Wright treated the property like a natural garden and developed a series of paths through it, each leading to some special place, following the model of linking the house to the quarry-turned-lake. In an essay he wrote in 1970 he outlined the techniques he used and what he learned from the approach of developing "a garden of woodland paths." In it, he suggests making themed paths such as a morning path leading east so a walker can admire the sun shining through the trees, or a winter path to take advantage of evergreen plants. He developed paths to show off the most interesting features of his land and then carefully gardened by subtraction, removing trees gradually to open up vistas to borrowed landscapes and to create gathering spaces within the woods.

Wharton Esherick (1887–1970), an American artist-craftsman, built his rectangular stone studio and shop along the crest of Valley Forge Mountain in Paoli, Pennsylvania. His artistic work includes paintings, woodcuts, wood sculptures, furniture, and interior design. At the New York World's Fair in 1940, his work, including the spiral staircase from his Paoli studio, was featured in a model interior of "a Pennsylvania Hill House." He built and developed his home-studio, which today is a National Historic Landmark and serves as the Wharton Esherick Museum, over a forty-year period, from 1926 to 1966.

From the outside the house-studio resembles a Pennsylvania bank barn, set on the slope of a hill with a simple rectangular form. The exposed elements of the house, made primarily of local fieldstone and cedar, blend with the wooded property. A tower added to the basic structure in 1941 is referred to as a silo, and its shape and materials borrow from the grain silos so frequently associated with

Wharton Esherick's home-studio in Paoli, Pennsylvania, borrows from vernacular architecture, although his barnlike building has ample windows to take in the natural beauty.

The juxtaposition of the garden pool and the dining room of this house on Mount Desert Island, Maine, along with its use of window walls, enables inhabitants to enjoy the garden while dining inside.

barns of the region. This vernacular form and the materials used help wed this house to its site.

From the inside, in both the studio and the dining room, large windows offer views to the outside. Upstairs, the built-in bed hugs a window the length of the bed from which there's an expansive view, as from a crow's nest, of the wooded hillside below. Throughout the interior Esherick used wood, mostly harvested from the property, to create furniture and fixtures. Walls are paneled with boards of cherry and oak. Sculptural shelves and irregularly cut floorboards are made from scraps of apple and walnut. Some pieces of furniture feature carved panels inspired by the views of the woods from the house, such as his drop-leaf desk decorated with carved branch patterns. The exquisite spiral staircase that connects the main floor to the loft is described in a pamphlet cataloging the museum (Aichele 1977) as "'tree form' with rough-hewn oak steps that project from a twisted Y-shaped trunk like the stubs of pruned branches." The handrails are made of smoothed bent branches. So a tree seems to be at the heart of this house, as it is at Dragon Rock, but in this case one even has a sense of climbing the tree as one climbs the spiral staircase to reach the upper floor.

If you do have the opportunity to build a house starting from the land, the lesson all three of these examples teach is: think about the marriage of the house to the land by determining where best to site the house to take advantage of views from the inside to the outside and to truly celebrate its unique features. The vast majority of houses built today are sited as though the most important aspect of their siting is how the house looks from the street or public point of view at the front of the house. The typical result is that the vast majority of windows, and hence the vast majority of views, are in the least rewarding direction—to a street or public promenade. From this orientation, you would think roads and parked cars were the best feature of the landscape to bring into view from the house. In all three of the celebrated examples just described, the houses are oriented or linked to the natural features of the property so the inhabitants can best enjoy and take in the beauty of the setting.

Although most of us probably won't have the opportunity to acquire substantial acreage and build our own houses, the three example properties nevertheless offer lessons to employ or adapt to modern-day suburban-sized or even urban-sized settings to enhance the link between the inside and the outside. Even if you start with a pre-existing house sited in the traditional mode, with its sides parallel with the sides of the lot, you can still successfully bring the outside inside in a number of ways, as outlined next.

ROOMS WITH VIEWS

Take your drapes down. I have no curtains on my windows, even though I live in the middle of town with close neighbors on all sides. It's one of the most economical and effective ways of immersing myself in the garden even while I'm indoors. But I do have privacy; my "curtains" consist of trees and shrubs planted around my small lot. From the dining room table, the east-facing window frames a view of a mature American holly; the double windows to the south, even though they're just a few feet from the street and overlook my driveway, are filled with a view of the branches of a black locust from one side and sumac from the other. Soothing green leaves block my view of the street while also shading the house during the growing season. The windows in the living room frame snapshot views of viburnums and a franklinia; a window in the bedroom allows me to wake up and frequently observe mourning doves drinking from a birdbath while I'm still in bed. From the north-facing bedroom window I appreciate the handsome culms of a black bamboo set off against a fence. The bamboo effectively screens my view from a close neighbor on that side and permits me not to constantly pull the blind. My windows function like picture frames, capturing views into the garden or plants in the garden. Granted, while these views are not as spectacular as those at Fallingwater or Dragon Rock, they offer natural beauty on a daily basis. In effect the windows are the most prominent artwork in nearly every room of my house

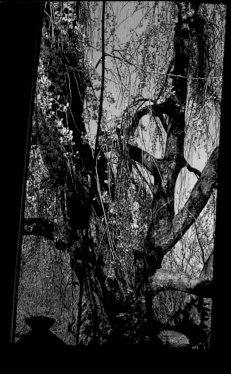

A three-paneled kitchen window takes on the feeling of a Japanese screen with this intimate view of a weeping Japanese cherry.

Without curtains, and with planting done with views in mind, windows can serve as effective portals to the garden, making the residents aware of seasonal changes such as the blooming of this eastern redbud (*Cercis canadensis*).

The front door of the lodge at Asticou Gardens, on Mount Desert Island, Maine, provides a strong connection to the elements of the garden with natural stone forming the entry walkway and with arborvitae trunks serving as a focal point.

and certainly the most dynamic, since I can easily observe seasonal changes and events in the garden as part of my daily routine.

Walk through your house looking outside from every window. Does the view make a good picture? Are you missing an opportunity because you've blocked the view with shades and curtains or overgrown foundation plants? Even if you don't have a waterfall, a forest, or a quarry, you can create a beautiful view to a single

By enclosing a portion of this side garden, the owners have created an outside room that maintains some privacy while they enjoy the garden.

tree, simple planting, created water feature, or stone composition. By developing as many unique views to the outside as you can, you'll enrich the moods and emotions of the connections from the inside to the outside, just as Russel Wright varied the moods of his garden walks.

Add windows and doors to provide more portals to the outside. Who says you have to stick with the small, sparse, evenly spaced windows you inherited with your ranch-style house? A small in-town house I once lived in had no door on the back opening to the garden. There was a front door and a side door off the driveway, but adding a door to a room on the back of the house dramatically increased my connection to the enclosed back garden and the time I spent in it.

Because Americans still build and maintain their suburban properties as though a law exists that the full frontal view of the house must be offered to all who pass or drive by, our front lawns are de facto public spaces. They become a no-man's-land seldom crossed by anyone other than the mail carrier or pizza delivery person. Rarely are they used for living in or for the edification of those who reside within. Reclaiming this space as part of the landscape to be enjoyed by and inhabited by the homeowner can improve the connection of the house to the site and enhance the quality of living. By planting at or near the perimeter of the property or by enclosing it within fences or walls, you can make the space belong to or be oriented to the house versus the road and strangers beyond, and the views from the rooms on the front of the house will consist of more than a sterile field of mowed lawn.

This composition of redbuds and boulders provides beautiful views out toward the sidewalk from the generous windows and doors of this Salt Lake City residence.

The front lawn of this Salt Lake City residence has been planted with views from the inside in mind. It's not the typical suburban barren expanse of lawn that provides full disclosure of the house to strangers.

PORCHES

Porches are where the inside and the outside obviously mingle. I live in a small bungalow with a generous open-air front porch that spans nearly the full length of the façade. Having lived with this space for some time now, I have a hard time imagining giving up this special area that so easily connects my house and my living patterns to the outside. As soon as the days turn mild, I frequently take breakfasts and dinners outside, sitting in the old-fashioned porch swing to enjoy both morning and evening light on the garden while I eat. I edited this book while I was swinging there. Even on rainy days, I can enjoy the porch because of its wide overhang. From there I can admire the progression of bloom and growth throughout the spring, summer, and fall. I've even spied hummingbirds gathering nectar just a few feet away before alighting on the river birches for a rest. Only when the dropping temperature dictates do I reluctantly move back inside.

My grandparents had a screened-in porch situated on the side of their farmhouse, where its structure didn't interfere with views to the outside landscape from the interior rooms on the front and back of the house. From the porch, they could take in panoramic views of the surrounding farm fields (that is, until wisteria engulfed one side). This became the room of choice for meals and conversation during the growing season. One door connected it to the kitchen, another to the dining room, making the outdoors one step away from these rooms.

Add a porch if your house doesn't have one, whether open-air or screened-in. A house without a porch lacks a space where the inside and the outside come to-

A front porch on a shingle-style house in Baltimore offers different garden vignettes through each pair of columns.

This screened-in porch offers a dramatic overview of the garden while providing a comfortable place to dine and relax outside.

gether readily. Porchless houses remind me of the box-shaped house tokens from the game of Monopoly. Such houses, like the Monopoly tokens, seem like they could be picked up and put down anywhere, because they have no connection to the outdoors. If you already have a porch, don't enclose it to expand your house. Though frequently done as an easy way to gain more interior square footage, expanding the walls of the house to consume porch areas means you'll sacrifice having the outside embraced or welcomed in. Turning screen to glass can make a

The broad front porch on this Victorian house encourages lingering outside to take in views of the garden while providing comfortable protection from the elements.

Porches are places where the house and the garden mingle, particularly true in this case since the main peak of the house extends into the landscape to form the porch roof and the porch supports are planted in the garden on the far end.

summer porch into a year-round porch, but turning screen to drywall blocks off the outdoors from the house.

The lack of any kind of front porch or overhang also explains why some front doors are rarely, if ever, used. They don't provide for a comfortable transition from the outside to the inside. If you have to stand in the rain while you juggle an umbrella and shopping bags and try to find the door key, why would you use this front door, when a side door or back door or door through the garage provides protection from the elements?

TERRACES AND DECKS

Terraces and decks are places where the inside protrudes outside. While they may facilitate our spending pleasurable time outside, just as porches do, they can also create greater distance between the inside and the outside if they're not carefully planned. If French doors that once opened directly into the garden and framed a garden view now open onto a deck cluttered with furniture, the inside has been distanced from the outside. In adding porches, decks, and terraces, evaluate the importance of the views from individual windows and doors to minimize the loss of intimacy with the garden. Add these features only where they won't interfere with the best views to the outside from the heart of the house.

A couple I know built a house in New Jersey with a dramatic wall of windows and doors to allow a view into the natural woods covering a hill immediately behind the house. In the fall, the reds, oranges, yellows, and greens of maple, oak, and sumac fill the living room with dramatic intensity. It feels as though you can

Decks that accommodate dining and socializing blur the distinction between the inside and the outside. In this garden on Bainbridge Island, Washington, created by Dan Hinkley and Robert Jones, shade cloth can be drawn to provide shade if needed.

In California, the dry, mild climate makes it possible to take the kitchen outside as a garden room.

The outside and the inside are brought together with this small patio in a Seattle garden.

reach right out the window and collect brightly colored leaves. Adding a deck or terrace outside that window would compromise this sense of connection between the inside and the outside; the couple would be looking through railings and at outdoor furniture for much of the year instead of at the trees.

SOFTENING EDGES

Add planters, containers, and window boxes to help blur the sharp line between the inside and the outside, and to soften the delineation of a deck from the garden. If you page through any of the numerous books documenting Frank Lloyd Wright's work, you'll see many examples of containers designed as part of the architecture and as a way of bringing plants right up to or even inside the house. The Fallingwater planters fall half inside and half outside the window walls. At the Coonley Residence, a Frank Lloyd Wright house in Riverside, a section of Chicago, ferns grow outside the dining room window in a combination wall and raised planter. From the dining room table, one has the sensation of looking out into the forest floor even though the dining room is at a raised elevation. This

The dramatic view from this living room means the residents can admire seasonal changes and the beauty of the woods on a daily basis. They wisely refrained from adding a terrace or deck that would have distanced the trees from the heart of the house.

planter-wall also allows Virginia creeper to cascade over the façade of the house, further tying together the elements of the house and the garden. Walls that double as planters are part of Wright's Willits House in Highland Park, Illinois, his May House in Grand Rapids, Michigan, his Hollyhock House and Storer House, both in Los Angeles, and his Honeycomb House in Palo Alto, California, to name a few. Wright-designed container-planters have been reproduced, just as his furniture has been, since they were such an important design element in his work.

Just as walls can double as planters, so can steps. At Sir John Thouron's garden in Unionville, Pennsylvania, broad stone stairs leading from a terrace outside the house down to the garden below double as a tough garden. Tread stones missing from the sides of the grand semicircular stairs create planting pockets, allowing dainty choice plants to be dramatically displayed while they in turn soften the stone and lighten the effect of the staircase in the garden. At Chanticleer in Wayne, Pennsylvania, the railing of another set of stone steps doubles as a raised planter. You can't help but notice the plants near eye level and brush some of them with your hand as you make your way down the staircase holding the handrail. At the Gamble House in Pasadena, California, creeping fig (*Ficus pumila*) growing on the face of the risers of the prominent steps leading up to the front door unites the entrance with the garden.

Similarly, if you're building a stone or brick terrace, patio, or walkway, consider leaving gaps or planting pockets and laying the material in dry sand instead of concrete so this area, too, can bloom like a garden. In a small patio I laid in dry sand, I added bluets (*Hedyotis caerulea*) in small pockets. Ultimately they filled the cracks among all of the stones, creating a magical pattern in bloom while remaining small enough for the area to continue to function comfortably to sit and dine in. In my current garden, native coral bells (*Heuchera americana*) and foamflower (*Tiarella cordifolia*) grow here and there among the stones and bricks of outdoor terrace areas, having spread on their own. In another example, at the Scott Arboretum of Swarthmore College, the plaza/terrace areas of a residence hall have borders where sedum was interplanted among stones laid into gravel. Stones mingle with plants and the walkways gradually turn into part of the garden with this treatment.

Extend the paving material of your garden walkways into the entrance foyer or other rooms of your house. Brick, flagstone, concrete, and tiles can work both outside and inside if carried across the threshold. The material can provide visual continuity as you pass from the garden into the house, making the transition less abrupt. At the Scott Arboretum, the flagstone used in the Cosby Courtyard forms the floor of the lobby that looks out onto the garden. To those sitting in the lobby and looking out through the expansive glass walls, the stone appears to be continuous and unites the two spaces visually. At the Coonley Residence, the earth-colored concrete leading from the street to the entrance of the house continues inside to form an entry hall. After that transition, a few concrete steps rise to connect to the level of the wood floors. In both of these examples, the grade of

Architectural aspects of a house such as walls and steps can blend with the garden if they become part planter. The example of Sir John Thouron's garden steps can be modified to use on a smaller scale.

Softening these natural boulders with plants in the cracks brings nature right up to the back door of this home on Martha's Vineyard.

A trellised walkway off the drive leads visitors through the garden to the front door of this California house, making the act of approaching the house feel like a garden journey.

the garden is the same as the immediate interior spaces, making the flow between the two especially smooth.

Similarly, use building material inside that represents the outside. A tree trunk such as the one that became a support post at Dragon Rock or a staircase in Wharton Esherick's home can become a coatrack inside the front door or serve as a banister handrail, a base for a coffee table, a stool to sit on, or countless other items. Furniture and fixtures made of natural materials found outside the front door blur the distinctions between the inside and the outside. These pieces don't have to be rustic in character. The refined and revered furniture of George Nakashima that celebrates the life of each tree the piece was made from, brings an awareness of natural processes to the act of eating or sitting while inside. Using garden furniture as interior furniture blurs the distinction in a whimsical and economical way. Substitute a poolside chaise longue for a recliner chair or bring in a birdbath and cover its basin with glass to form an end table.

Plant vines or train espaliers against your house walls to soften the transition from garden to building and to connect the built structure to the landscape. On my small bungalow, four different vines soften corners, connect porch pillars to plantings, or cloak part of the stucco walls. On the front porch, Dutchman's pipe (*Aristolochia macrophylla*) twines around the stone porch pillar on one side, while kiwi (*Actinidia kolomikta*) does so on the other side. On the back of the house,

Japanese hydrangea vine (*Schizophragma hydrangeoides*) wraps around one corner of the small room that juts out into the garden, and silver-vein creeper (*Parthenocissus henryana*) softens the corner by the back door, where it has run across the steps and climbed up the stucco walls. The four vines help embrace the house in a way that makes it feel well connected to and integrated with the small garden, and each vine offers a different habit and seasonal interest, much of which I can view through windows.

Allow a tree to remain in a walkway or plant one to poke up through a deck or a terrace. A house I lived in in Swarthmore, Pennsylvania, looked out into woods that covered a slope down to Crum Creek. A raised deck on the house encircled a tulip tree, whose trunk was accommodated by a generous hole cut into the deck boards. In this way the house seemed to honor the woods, and every time I ventured onto the deck, I noticed the furrowed bark of that tulip tree in a way I would not have if it hadn't been central to the deck.

Add a pergola or a trellised walkway or sitting area such as a gazebo. Such structures create spaces where the solidness of the house gradually gives way to the openness of the garden. Trellised walkways can soften the edges of the house, and gazebos are destinations to visit, encouraging a walk through the garden. A small sitting area in the back of my garden also serves as a place to enjoy summer dinners. A simple rectangular wooden structure with lath sides creates a sense of an outside dining room. Its walls are partially cloaked with another Dutchman's pipe vine.

And think earth colors. White houses don't blend with their surroundings, and white picket fences and red barns, while traditional, make a statement of separation from their natural settings. A house painted a moss color or the color of stone or sand harmonizes with the garden rather than contrasting with it, and its presence seems to diminish, allowing your eye to go to the landscape and not get stuck on the house.

FURTHER EXAMPLES FROM PUBLIC SPACES

It's worth mentioning some examples beyond residences that further illustrate this principle to show that it's possible to tie rooms and buildings and spaces intended to serve hundreds or even thousands of people to nature and the outdoors. A number of performance spaces across the country follow this principle. At the Santa Fe Opera House, an audience of thousands can enjoy performances in the open-air theater while also enjoying the evening air and the view of surrounding mountains. At the Frank Gehry–designed stage and accompanying lawn in Millennium Park, opened in 2004, thousands can sit on the lawn, listen to the Chicago Symphony, and gaze at the dramatic Chicago skyline.

At Longwood Gardens in Kennett Square, Pennsylvania, the Open Air Theater provides another opportunity to have grass underfoot and views of trees while enjoying the performing arts. In this instance, sidewalls are composed of clipped

The stage window wall of the Lang Music Building at Swarthmore College ensures that members of the audience are visually entertained by views into the eastern deciduous woods while they're also entertained with musical performances.

arbor vitae hedges, and rather than dropping from a ceiling, the final curtain rises up from the stage—a row of water jets shoots up from the stage floor and is hit with bright lights that effectively turn the fountain into a water curtain.

At the Scott Arboretum, the Scott Outdoor Amphitheater is a marvelous example of designing in harmony with nature and bringing the indoors outdoors. The amphitheater is set on a natural slope and has a high ceiling provided by the

The Scott Outdoor Amphitheater at Swarthmore College in Pennsylvania is a stunning example of building in harmony with nature and fusing activities generally associated with indoor spaces to a spectacular natural setting.

leaves and branches of native tulip trees (*Liriodendron tulipifera*) that randomly rise up from the stepped, stone-faced tiers that were added to the hillside. Some of the trees punctuate the stone bands, since they existed before the tiers were constructed. The tiers and the stage are carpeted with lawn. Beyond the stage, which is also formed by fieldstone walls, the audience looks into mature eastern deciduous woods of ash, tulip trees, oak, and maple back-lit by the sun in the evenings. Although the space holds as many as 2500 people for formal commencement ceremonies, it feels intimate and hidden from view due to its being set in the woods in such a sensitive manner. American holly, rhododendron, hemlock, and spruce surround it, making it feel like you've discovered a secret place in the forest upon entering it, even though it's only a short distance from buildings on campus.

Next door to this amphitheater, the Lang Music Building serves as another inspired example of this principle. A traditional indoor concert hall manages to take

In Pasadena, California, this grand entrance to the Norton Simon Museum embraces the landscape, with the trees that remain in the walkway and the glassed-in entry room that keeps visitors' eyes focused on the garden even after they've entered the building. The garden's designer, Nancy Goslee Power, placed the trees in the walkway to create a gateway to the museum and cause visitors to pause.

the audience into the same woods because the back wall of the stage is a window wall framing a view into the woods. No service roads, loading docks, or walkways obscure the view. Concert attendees come to hear music but they're visually transported into nature simultaneously in either of these spaces.

In Camden, Maine, at the public library, an outdoor amphitheater designed by Fletcher Steele relies upon stone tiers and a canopy of white-barked birches in a similar vein to the Scott Outdoor Amphitheater. The U-shaped tiers face the Camden harbor, so beyond the performance area, the view is of picturesque boats and docks.

Performances in any of these spaces that tie the inside to the outside become occasions not just for enjoying the performing arts but also for communing or connecting with nature and the seasons.

The inside can still be married to the outside even when the residence has no land, as demonstrated by landscape architect Dennis McGlade's rooftop garden, which provides a dramatic view of the Philadelphia skyline as borrowed scenery.

Perhaps the ultimate examples of living with an awareness of the landscape come from ancient times. Hollowed-out yew trees in the British Isles became quaint one-room hermitages; stone structures overhung by cliffs served as the dwellings of the Anasazi Indians in the Southwest; caves in Southern Spain were used as abodes by gypsies. I hope the examples in this chapter have shown you that there are many ways to live in closer relationship to the outdoors that are more practical and readily accessible than seeking out a cave, a cliff dwelling, or a tree stump to live in.

5

Involve the Visitor

MUSEUM CURATORS have effectively developed sophisticated interactive exhibits through the last two decades to engage museum visitors in all kinds of ways and in all types of activities. No longer do museums seem like warehouses full of glass cases stuffed with artifacts identified with only basic labels. Audio devices allow us to hear directly from the curator as though we were taking a private tour. Drawers can be pulled out to see additional specimens or artifacts, computer screens can be touched or video clips played to see how the object on display was made or used. Mini-theaters within the exhibits play movies to further supplement our understanding and appreciation of the artist, collection on view, or culture pertaining to the exhibit. "Please touch" signs are now almost as common as "don't touch" signs. Curators have applied the knowledge that the more visitors become engaged in the exhibit, physically and sensually, the more they learn.

While we don't design or consider our backyard Edens or even most of our public gardens as museum exhibits, the same concept applies. If you want to affect people—relax them, recharge them, enrich them, delight them, educate them—with your garden, engage them physically and mentally. Involve the visitor in the garden. Like the audience invited to clap their hands at a concert, visitors need to participate in experiencing your garden if they're going to be moved by its "music." So this is the fifth principle. The more you and your visitors touch, smell, hear, and see in the garden, the more profound and transformative the garden's effect.

ENGAGING ATTENTION THROUGH THE FEET

One of the reasons Japanese gardens resonate so strongly with so many, I suspect, is that these gardens successfully engage the visitor. A Japanese stroll garden with stepping-stones or a zigzag plank bridge over open water requires you to devote attention to where you're stepping. Stepping-stones also dictate the size of your step; they control the experience of walking. To some degree, these methods of crossing water force you to notice the water at least momentarily. When your

Stepping-stones dictate the size of the steps a visitor takes in the garden created by Dan Hinkley and Robert Jones on Bainbridge Island, Washington. Such stepping-stones cause visitors to look at what lies underfoot—such as flowing water—with greater attention and awareness than solid paths or bridges would.

This footbridge, connecting to a remnant of a dead tree, engages the garden visitor in an event that happened in the garden—the life and death of the tree.

The stepping-stones in the Elisabeth Carey Miller Botanical Garden in Seattle, Washington, draw visitors' attention to the ground covers and low shrubs interspersed among them.

Stepping-stones over running water in a courtyard at Grounds for Sculpture in Hamilton, New Jersey, bring visitors close to a dramatic garden feature.

A garden path at a residence in Menlo Park, California, forces visitors to step over open water, which may give them pause for thought.

A path in the Garfield Park Conservatory, Chicago, Illinois, designed by Jens Jensen, engages visitor interest.

A path interrupted by boulders also causes visitors to stop and ponder their next step and notice elements of the landscape.

At the Missouri Botanic Garden in St. Louis, crossing these stepping-stones engages visitors in the pool and the patterns of the water.

thoughts and attention are directed to the garden, thoughts of the outside world you brought into the garden are effectively displaced; you're engaged in the garden and its elements. The garden becomes a form of meditation due to its physical aspects.

In traditional Chinese gardens, paths were laid out in a zigzag pattern with the intention of directing and controlling visitors' views of features in the garden. Many design approaches used in Japanese and Chinese stroll gardens to engage visitors aren't culturally dependent. The same approach can be used elsewhere with the same effect on the visitor. It isn't the Japanese stones placed in the water or the Japanese lumber of the footbridge that determines their success; it's their relationship to the water and how they allow the visitor to experience the water that's the critical lesson they teach us. Stepping over a root, ducking under a low branch, feeling the coolness of a spray of water all heighten a visitor's awareness of the garden or aspects of it in universal ways.

THE GARDEN AS A SEQUENCE OF DISCOVERY

The idea that a garden should be walked through as a choreographed or controlled experience or as a journey of discovery, perfected in Japan, works just as well in the development of a Western garden. Lawns randomly punctuated with flower beds or specimen trees offer no invitation to experience the space other than by scanning it visually. After your eye has bounced from bed to bed, you have "seen the garden"; there's nothing to pull you closer into or through the garden. When you develop your garden as a journey, a stroll garden, moving through the space becomes a sequence of experiences of discovery and engagement. A path acts as a way to orchestrate the experiences by directing us, leading us, teaching us, and it piques our curiosity when it disappears into the woods, through a hedge, or around a corner. A well-designed path pulls us mentally and physically. It determines our views of the garden and the order in which parts of the garden are revealed to us.

Even on a small urban lot, garden paths can direct and encourage a visitor's experience and create a sense of journey. The path that essentially circles my bungalow gives me a sense of discovery every time I make the loop around. Arriving home by car, I'm led by a turf path a few feet wide from my parking spot through mixed borders up to the front door. Off the traditional straight walkway connecting my front door to the street, a narrow turf path continues around to the north side of the house. It passes through river birches and hydrangeas, then disappears through an opening formed by the branches of flanking cryptomerias. On the other side of the opening, a grove of black bamboo is revealed, lining the path that now runs parallel to the side of the house in the limited band I have to garden there. A series of square flagstone stepping-stones, set in gray pea gravel, create a strong pattern to pull my focus downward, thereby diverting attention from the three-story house next door. The path turns around the back corner of the house and opens into the shady back garden of perennials, shrubs, a few small trees, and sitting areas for al fresco dining. Continuing on around, at the other back corner of the house the path goes through a garden gate and down steps to the driveway/parking space.

With large properties, and in public gardens, there's a tendency to develop a maze of paths, but a network of paths doesn't guarantee greater engagement. Having a path lead you through a garden, the way a well-designed museum exhibit takes you on a course to enhance learning, means you are never left bewildered, wondering which way to go. The less time you spend deciphering a map or worrying and wondering which path to take, the more time you spend looking at and absorbing the elements of the garden.

One of the most memorable American stroll gardens I've visited is Innisfree in Millbrook, New York. The garden celebrates rural New York's rolling hills, pastures, and ponds, although the garden makers were deeply influenced by Chinese stroll gardens. The circular path around the lake provides a clearly defined journey, which becomes a well-orchestrated sequence of discoveries as it reveals views and surprising moments such as a water geyser tucked into an alcove of the pond or a corncrib converted into a footbridge over a seepage area or a rock outcropping where water mist creates a white spray among the rocks. The original mansion proved too costly to maintain as a part of the property; if you stand where it once stood, you get a sweeping view of the lake but just a glimpse of the path and few if any of the unique moments you can only discover by walking through the garden.

Another memorable example of a distinctly American stroll garden is Chanticleer in Wayne, Pennsylvania, which like Innisfree was developed as a private garden and is now open to the public. In this case it was the process of turning it into a public garden that provided the impetus for adding a circular pathway in a choreographed manner. The garden today is composed of what had been three separate residences. To unify the residences, garden areas, and distinct destinations, a macadam pathway edged with cobblestones was added. The path serves as the line to connect the dots of garden features; it strings interesting areas together like beads in a necklace. It leads the visitor unambiguously through courtyards and terraces, down hills, around ponds, along a stream, and back to the beginning point. Along the way the guest discovers springhouses, ruins, bridges, sitting areas, vistas, woods, and exuberant plantings. Where there are expanses of lawn and open spaces, the path defines the course to take where none would otherwise be suggested, providing the structure to keep the visitor from randomly bouncing about and perhaps missing some of the garden features. The path allows visitors to enjoy the sense of discovery and journey and frees them from the need to navigate as well as any Japanese or Chinese stroll garden does. Although Chanticleer and Innisfree are smaller in acreage than many other public gardens in this country, they have become favorites with visitors, I would argue because of the strongly defined way both gardens allow visitors to experience them.

PHYSICAL INVOLVEMENT BEYOND STROLLING

Creating slightly challenging physical aspects along the way provides hooks to engage visitors. As mentioned, stepping-stones over open water control the size of your step, where you step, and where you'll look if you're going to avoid falling in. The thoughts in your head when you came into the garden are pushed out as you focus on the challenge before you in order to continue on your journey.

At Mount Cuba Center, the naturalistic native plant garden in Hockessin, Delaware, where I worked, I had the chance to observe how such garden features shape our experiences. At the top of a valley of four man-made ponds, the path crosses over a small "stream" connecting two of the ponds and requires visitors to step across the open water on stones placed on both sides of the spillway. At that point visitors consistently pause before meeting the small challenge of crossing the water since only one at a time can pass on the stepping-stones. It gives members

In Frank Cabot's garden in Quebec, Canada, visitors are physically engaged when they cross a swinging rope bridge spanning a valley in the garden. The need to travel single file across the bridge ensures that they will be alone with the garden at least for the time it takes them to cross the bridge.

A narrow path resembling a deer trail in this Connecticut garden of the late Linc and Timmy Foster forces visitors to slow down and watch their step, and thereby notice the dainty flowers of creeping phlox along the way.

Providing opportunities to sit, lie down, or swing invites visitors to linger, notice, and enjoy the garden in a way other than just passing through it—it encourages engagement and involvement.

of a party time to look up and around, and thereby notice the view down through the valley to the pond below, before they decide to step across the stream. It slows them down, causing them to take note of one of the most beautiful vistas in the garden. It also means each of them becomes alone with the garden, if just for the brief moment it takes them to individually step across the stream on those two stones, and in that moment they look at the flow of the water and perhaps hear its gurgling sounds. This kind of intimate contact and awareness makes a garden memorable; it lets the garden perform its transformative magic.

Earlier I described garden furniture as an example of how to derive beauty from function. I mention garden furniture again here as an example of how to accomplish this principle. Providing places to sit, to eat, to sleep, to lounge invites people into the garden and engages them in those activities while surrounded by the garden. At the Scott Arboretum, several dozen classic white Adirondack chairs reside on a broad open lawn area. While they're pleasing to look at when no one is sitting in them—the "furniture as sculpture" concept—they also allow and encourage people to sit in what might be regarded as an uninviting or uninteresting open space. Visitors or students sitting there resting, eating lunch, or reading surely notice the huge swamp white oaks, the sky, and the sloping lawn more profoundly than when just walking by.

Beyond designing physically engaging aspects in your garden, stimulate as many of the senses as possible. Although we tend to focus on sight, thinking of gardens as a primarily visual art form, no other kind of art provides so many possibilities to engage so many senses simultaneously. There are unique opportunities to delight all the senses in the garden—touching, smelling, hearing, and seeing.

TOUCHING

Adding "please touch" signs may be an appropriate way in public gardens to get visitors to feel the softness of lamb's ears, but intimate contact with plants in both private and public gardens can also be successfully orchestrated in subtler ways. Planting fountains of ornamental grasses along walkways or outlining narrow paths almost guarantees that visitors will reach out and run their hands along the grasses' leaves or seed heads, for example.

Visiting the restored prairies in the University of Wisconsin Landscape Arboretum, I observed how a busy, chattering group of people once led onto a path that amounted to no more than a deer trail became a quieter single file of walkers since the path didn't accommodate walking two or more abreast. And then, no longer separated from the herbs and grasses by other people, each person had an unobstructed view into the prairie and couldn't help being brushed by native plants spilling over the pathways.

In Yvonne England's Pennsylvania country garden, a path leads through the branches of an old weeping willow. She has intentionally not cut the pendulous

Grasses spilling over the simple path around this small urban garden in Towson, Maryland, touch garden strollers as they discover distinct planting combinations on each side of the house.

Walkers along this garden path in Nutley, New Jersey, come into gentle, direct contact with the inflorescences of ornamental grasses.

The pathway in Yvonne England's garden leads visitors through a curtain of weeping willow branches. Visitors are engaged through a sense of touch when they part the branches, like parting a bead curtain in a doorway. The branches swaying in the gentlest of breezes also provide animation in the garden.

branches away, which would have been the tendency of many people in order to make mowing and walking easier. Passing through this portion of her garden is like stepping through a stage curtain, and it encourages touching the willow's supple branches.

In another residential garden I've experienced, the cascading branches of a weeping cherry tree planted near a path envelop visitors—truly a magical experience when the branches are in bloom. I've also admired weeping forms of blue atlas cedars trained to form an arch or doorway with a curtain of branches, encouraging visitors to notice and perhaps feel the prickly needles on the branches while walking through the garden.

The sense of touch in the garden can also be powerfully engaged with the use of water. Provide a way for people to dangle their hands in a curtain of water or play with the water jets of a fountain or be close enough to feel the mist or spray from water and you'll delight them with a sensory experience particularly appreciated on hot summer days. I've admired how a small water feature that creates a veil of water with a single jet set in a flowerpot filled with black stones mesmerized visitors in a small urban garden. Visitors found it hard to walk by the feature

In a small walled garden in Wayne, Pennsylvania, the pendulous branches of a weeping cherry surround a visitor up close with cherry blossoms in the spring, cooling foliage and shade in the summer, and bare wiry branches in the winter.

Visitors have a hard time not playing with the veil of water generated by this simple water feature right at arm's length.

At Grounds for Sculpture in Hamilton, New Jersey, a water feature sprays like a shower from a wall over several boulders, encouraging visitors to feel the mist or stick a hand or foot into the shower. The feature engages the senses of sight, hearing, and touch.

and not stick their fingers in the veil of water. In the Laurie Garden of Millennium Park, in Chicago, a channel of flowing water passes along a walkway with a sunken edge for sitting where weary strollers remove their shoes and dangle their feet, a sensory experience welcomed by residents and tourists during Chicago's hot summer days.

SMELLING

Brushing against plants engages the sense of touch in the garden, and it might also engage the sense of smell, depending on the plant. I delight in having clary sage (*Salvia sclarea*) at the edge of paths, where with a sweep of my hand over its leaves or flower stalks I can perfume the air with a pungent, awakening aroma. *Comptonia peregrina*, the sweet fern, a native eastern shrub, would do likewise. Boxwoods in traditional formal gardens planted along paths yield fragrances as well, though less enjoyable to my nose. Female ginkgos or the Chinese toon tree planted in your garden may cause you to retreat from the unpleasant smells of their fruits and flowers.

Lilacs, peonies, irises, roses, and some viburnums offer floral fragrances so pleasurable and intense that they leave lasting imprints on us. The trick to make that happen is to place these plants close to a patio, or by the mailbox, or along a path used during daily routines, so that even when we're harried, we get a whiff and then at least momentarily enjoy the garden through our olfactory glands. We "stop to smell the flowers" without taking up too much time.

Less traditional and obvious plants can be used to perfume the air at unexpected times or in unexpected ways. When *Sarcococca hookerana*, sweet box, blooms in late winter or early March in the Philadelphia region, its small white flowers held close to its stems go unnoticed but its powerful, sweet fragrance perfumes the air at a time of year when you least expect it. *Magnolia virginiana*, the sweet bay magnolia, blooms sporadically over a long period during the summer, and on still days its perfume will hang in the air. If the tree is placed near an entry patio or swimming pool terrace, its wonderful citrus-y fragrance can stump people as they search for the source of the perfume.

HEARING

The sound of catbirds repeating their varied and intricate melodies pulls me into my garden perhaps even before I'm ready on spring days when they start singing at daybreak. And in August, it isn't possible for me to block the sounds of the garden out—a constant humming, clicking, and chirping rings in my ears from the insects outside, especially since I don't close my windows or have the drone of an air conditioner drowning the sounds of the garden at that time of year. These gifts from the garden are largely beyond our control, although the way we tend our gardens can encourage or discourage these serendipitous sounds of nature. Add a small pool or pond to your garden and you'll likely be rewarded with spring peepers or the croaks of bullfrogs. Add birdbaths and feeders and you'll likely be rewarded with the songs of birds.

To engage the sense of hearing, water can again provide abundant opportunities. The sound of water can soothe our souls and get us to focus on elements in the garden, whether the sound comes from the dripping of a small water feature or from the flow of a dramatic waterfall. If the sound of water in the garden penetrates into the interior of your house, like my bird and insect sounds, the garden never seems far away and is always contributing to the experience of living through the sound it provides. Recall Fallingwater.

As mentioned in the second chapter, there's a unique garden artifact in Japan revered for the melancholy sound it generates, a device that originally served as a scarecrow. To review, the scarecrow consists of a length of bamboo several nodes

This simple jet of water, captured in a plastic barrel sunk into the ground and recirculated with a small pump, adds a visually engaging focal point with its movement and a refreshing sound amplified by the less-than-full barrel.

In this Phoenix, Arizona, garden, the sound of gurgling water penetrates into the bedroom through the screen doors, meaning the sounds of the garden are ever present to those inside the house. The sight and sound of water adds a cooling feeling in the dry, hot climate of the Southwest.

long with one end cut on an angle; the piece is balanced on a stand like a seesaw, near its midpoint so that the open cut end is up in the resting position. The stand is placed in the garden in such a way that a trickle of water drips into the cut, hollow section of the bamboo. As water fills the upper section, it becomes top-heavy and tips on the stand, allowing the water to flow out. Now empty of water, the bamboo seesaws back to the original position, at which moment it hits a rock strategically placed beneath the low end and makes a bonking sound, originally intended to scare wildlife away. Every time the sequence is repeated, a percussive sound resonates throughout the garden. Today such devices are added to gardens of all sizes, even pocket gardens gracing entries to restaurants on the seventh floor of Japanese department stores, purely for the sound and movement they provide.

The regular *bonk, bonk, bonk* sound of the Japanese scarecrow symbolizes the countryside or old rural Japan to the Japanese. Today, with such scarecrows used in unlikely locations, it's evident that they've evolved into a type of cherished water chime. In the last few years I've even seen plastic renditions of these Japanese

Japanese scarecrows are offered for sale in a department store gardening section.

scarecrows sold in American home stores as small garden water fountains, further showing the cross-cultural allure of the sound and movement these artifacts create in the garden.

Along these lines but in a culturally familiar way, at Mount Cuba Center a simple garden spigot atop a three-foot pipe was fashioned into a small water feature that adds a gentle dripping sound to the garden as water falls into a puddle rock placed as an ornamental catch basin. Yvonne England's millstone fountain, described in the second chapter, creates a similarly enticing sound in her garden.

Wind chimes and bells, other readily available ornaments, can also be added to the garden to create sound. But many produce annoying noise instead of soothing sounds, so evaluate the emotional impact of the sounds chimes and bells create before adding such features to your garden. The Paolo Soleri–designed bronze wind-bells cast in sand at Cosanti and Arcosanti in Arizona are examples of some notable garden ornaments designed to create sound.

Undesirable sounds such as traffic and air conditioning condensers may need to be masked to exclude them from your garden. A water feature that generates "white noise" can mitigate such unpleasant sounds. Recorded sounds might also be considered. I've been in several settings, such as tropical conservatories, where convincing frog, bird, or other animal noises are played to help create an awareness and appreciation of a distinct flora and its related fauna. Speakers disguised as rocks and boulders provide the means to add sounds of all types to outdoor settings without detracting from the beauty of the garden.

SEEING

The sense of sight is fundamental to our concepts of garden making since gardens are visual art forms, but gardens vary widely in their effectiveness at engaging the attention of those looking at them. The sense of sight is engaged through contrasting or harmonious colors and textures, and by varying the spaces created in gardens. Moreover, features adding motion are particularly compelling.

Certain plants, such as ornamental grasses, add animation to a garden, especially in the winter if they're not cut down. Even gentle breezes will sway their

Plantings of wildflowers and native trees provide a feast for the eyes of anyone following the naturalistic path of stepping-stones to enter this house in Newark, Delaware. And looking out the front door, the view is of dogwood instead of the street and parked cars.

leaves and feathery seed heads, creating a rustling sound. Animals—whether guinea hens, peacocks, sheep, or horses—also grab our attention because of their dynamic nature, as mentioned earlier in my discussion of "moving garden sculpture." Incorporating plants known to draw insects or birds is another way to assure that fleeting forms animate the garden, although not in an absolutely predictable way. Moving water is also visually engaging. Banners, flags, and fabrics dancing in the wind are other ways to add visual entertainment and a sense of animation. At Chanticleer, a waterwheel set in a stream running through the garden originally served to lift water to a tank for domestic use, although it was added more for ornament than function. It provides graceful, mesmerizing motion that commands your view and thoughts for some moments, and casts a calming effect as you stop to observe it.

The chairs in the open lawn spaces of the Scott Arboretum at Swarthmore College don't just encourage sitting and lingering in the area; they also provide a dynamic visual element in a large space that's otherwise rather static. Nearly every day the chairs move as those who sit in them take them from shade to sun or vice versa or form configurations to match the size of their party. (Students have literally turned the chairs into sculptural elements on April Fools' Day, stacking them into spires as a prank.) Although not as dynamic perhaps as moving water nor as picturesque as grazing Belted Galloways, the chairs provide a practical and useful way to add a dynamic visual quality to a simple landscape.

EVOKING A SENSE OF MYSTERY

Besides posing physical challenges and involving the senses, gardens can engage visitors by evoking a sense of mystery. A path leading around the corner of a house or through a hedge creates a sense of mystery by its disappearance and conjures up questions in the viewer's mind: Where does that go? What would I see if I were to follow that path? Creating curiosity powerfully engages and pulls visitors into a garden—both physically and mentally. Who hasn't had the experience of following a trail, a path, or a road that pulls you onward, curve after curve, as you say to yourself, I'll turn around after I see what's around the next bend?

Making "rooms" by dividing outdoor spaces with hedges, fences, or walls can also create a sense of mystery. Visitors want to step through the opening to see what's inside or revealed on the other side. The other advantage of dividing a garden into distinct spaces by using hedges or walls is that it makes the garden—especially if it's small—feel bigger. Visitors have the experience of discovering different spaces, and a sense of depth is enhanced by the partitions.

At Innisfree, the garden described earlier, one of the features visitors discover on their stroll-journey around the lake is an artistic composition of rock fragments held in a circular frame of carved stone set within a rock cliff. The composition

A sense of mystery is created with this misting fountain found on the campus of Harvard University in Boston. Those who explore or play in the mist are engaged with the sense of touch.

Arousing curiosity is a way to engage the mind of the visitor. Paths that lead around corners or through partial openings as in this urban Philadelphia garden tend to pull people through the garden because they wish to satisfy their curiosity about what lies beyond their immediate view.

appears to mask the mouth of a cave. You can't tell by viewing it what's behind it or how far the open space extends into the cliff, nor can you pass through it. It creates a sense of mystery that can't be dispelled, since entry isn't possible.

A similar sense of mystery is present in much of the stonework by Andy Goldsworthy, the British artist–sculptor who works only with elements he finds in nature. His work has been well documented in numerous books and the movie *Rivers and Tides*. His stone mounds, such as those now in the collection at the National Gallery in Washington, D.C., resemble igloos, each with a circular opening on the top. It's impossible to see into the black hole. These spaces, in essence black voids, I suspect engage us subconsciously with a sense of mystery. Looking into them, you feel as though you're looking into the black pupils of the eyes of another person.

Pools of black water create a similar sense of mystery, even if they're only a few feet in diameter. Without being able to see the bottom, viewers are left with unan-

An assemblage of rock by Andy Goldsworthy at Kentuck Knob near Pittsburgh, Pennsylvania, evokes a sense of mystery by creating an enclosed space; visitors are teased into stepping inside to experience the space and solve the mystery.

A rock composition at Innisfree evokes mystery by engaging visitors in pondering what they're witnessing.

Andy Goldsworthy's stonework at the Edinburgh Botanic Garden in Scotland creates a sense of mystery with its black hole that looks like the pupil of an eye.

swered questions and uncertainty. All these types of mysterious openings, to caves, to voids of space, to pools of water, affect us emotionally, tease us mentally, and make us stop to contemplate the garden or feature of the garden we're viewing.

At Manitoga, accounts persist that Russel Wright created at least one of his trails as though it petered out. Guests followed a well-defined path to a point where it unraveled among trees and rock outcroppings. There they had to look closely and search for clues to pick up the trail again. Across the boulder-punctu-

Fog generated by an in-ground irrigation system in a courtyard garden at Grounds for Sculpture creates a sense of mystery by momentarily obscuring views of the sculptures, other garden features, and fellow visitors.

ated glade, they would be funneled back onto a well-defined path with little real chance of becoming lost in the woods. Through this intentional design, Wright created a moment of uncertainty. Those on the path no doubt became engaged in the garden in an intent way as they studied the ground in efforts to "pick up the trail."

At Grounds for Sculpture in New Jersey, in an enclosed courtyard that displays various pieces of sculpture, an in-ground irrigation system creates a fine mist or fog, producing a visually changing composition and also a sense of mystery in the space. Fog intermittently fills the courtyard and obscures some of the sculpture, then disperses with a breeze. Sculptures, several of them of human forms, emerge from the fog and then are enshrouded once again. Similarly, in another part of the sculpture garden, mist created by nozzles blankets a pond, masking a bridge and a sculpture sited in the water in a continuously changing game of hide-and-reveal.

This giant frog waits as a surprise for visitors to discover after venturing down a garden path and can be prompted to croak with a little garden trickery.

CREATING SURPRISE

At Ashland Hollow, the residential garden of William and Nancy Frederick, one long pathway planted densely on either side with trees, shrubs, and perennials creates a silver-and-white-schemed allée. Lamb's ears, sea kale (*Crambe cordifolia*) with its clouds of small white flowers, and white-blooming rose-of-Sharon contribute to a serene summer scene. Toward the far end of the pathway a cluster of eastern red cedars provides a dark green backdrop to the composition and also serves to hide a surprise. Off to the side of the path, among the junipers, rests a giant frog sculpture that's revealed only when you're nearly upon it. More than six feet tall and at least as wide, the frog with its wide grin of a mouth is indeed a whimsical revelation. I've walked through the garden with guests guided by Bill Frederick where he encouraged a member of the group to kiss the frog, at which point the frog let out a "ribbit" or two (remotely controlled by Bill), although it failed to turn into a prince. So the first surprise is in discovering the giant frog, the second when it seems to come to life. Nothing engages visitors in a garden quite like the element of surprise. Creating a sense of surprise is akin to creating a sense of discovery in a stroll garden with more drama thrown in.

Spurting water features that catch visitors off guard have been developed by garden owners on small and grand scales to amuse and surprise garden visitors. Italian Renaissance water gardens are well known for grand water surprises. On a much smaller scale, a friend who goes only by the name of Simple created whimsical creatures from tubing and rubber caulking to do the same. He rigged them up with water features so that he could make them spit water on demand, to the delight, surprise, and engagement of his garden guests.

ADDING HUMOR

Besides adding the element of surprise, the hidden giant frog sculpture at Ashland Hollow also inevitably makes people laugh or at least smile back at the cartoonlike character with such a broad grin on its face. A sense of humor expressed in the garden can engage some visitors more raptly than visions of floral beauty.

In midlife, with no kids to provide an excuse, Richard Bitner, a serious gardener, added a tree house to his Pennsylvania farm-garden. After developing perennial borders, renovating ruins, laying his driveway with pavers, and completing many other projects a keen gardener would aspire to, he hired some builders to create a circular room around the trunk of a tulip tree a good thirty to forty feet above ground. It adds a sense of play to the garden and also reveals an enchanting view for those with enough agility and childlike sense of wonder to climb up the ladder into the tree house.

At Ladew Topiary Gardens, set amidst rolling hills in pastoral Monkton, Maryland, a number of beautiful and whimsical gardens were created by the original owner, Harvey Ladew. Visitors to what was a private garden in his day and is a public garden today first encounter a depiction of a foxhunt in progress. Yew beagles with all four feet extended fly after the frozen fox. This lighthearted caricature, though a demanding form of garden art, captures a scene from Ladew's life as a gentleman farmer and hunter in a humorous and endearing way.

The spectacular fountain-sculpture featured in Millennium Park in Chicago, refreshingly demonstrates humor on a grand public scale. Two glass-block pillars

A tree house for adults in Richard Bitner's garden invites visitors to see if they can meet the challenge of climbing the ladder. The reward, an aerial view of his Pennsylvania farm-garden, further engages visitors.

At Ladew Topiary Gardens in Maryland, a fox is forever being chased by hounds, bringing a sense of humor to the scene.

about the size of small city row houses face each other at either end of a shallow rectangular pool. A video of gigantic faces of Chicago citizens is projected onto the façades of the two pillars. The faces wink, smile, and gradually purse their lips as though they're going to blow a kiss. At that moment a gush of water spews out of the towers from their lips, as if a fire hydrant had been opened. Children run to stand in the stream of water, squealing with delight at being "spit on" by the giant faces. The sequence repeats with changing faces, delighting and engaging residents and tourists alike for hours on end, whether they get a shower or not.

Gardens, like life itself, are best enjoyed if they're not taken too seriously. Create a garden joke and you might successfully engage your visitors in a bit of garden laughter.

Make them laugh, make them cry, bemuse them, puzzle them—do all of this for your own pleasure as well as that of the visitors to your garden. Then, indeed, you've engaged them and given them something to feel, to delight in, and to reflect upon.

Faces projected on two glass-block pillars in Chicago's Millennium Park spew water at intervals in an endlessly entertaining and humorous display.

American Gardens Demonstrating These Principles

As EXAMPLES of the five principles, I've mentioned a number of public American gardens and landscapes—Manitoga, Fallingwater, Innisfree. In this chapter I describe how all five principles are played out in each of seven gardens. These gardens include three private residences and four public landscapes:

Private residential gardens

Longview Farm, the garden of the late Joanna Reed, Malvern, Pennsylvania

Ashland Hollow, the Frederick residence, Hockessin, Delaware

La Casita de Maria, the Frieder residence, Phoenix, Arizona

Public landscapes

The Brandywine Conservancy River Museum, Chadds Ford, Pennsylvania

The Crosby Arboretum, Picayune, Mississippi

The Lady Bird Johnson Wildflower Center, Austin, Texas

Superstition Springs Center, Mesa, Arizona

East and west, modest and major, all these gardens exhibit a strong American personality; they each fit their site and context.

Longview Farm, Malvern, Pennsylvania.

LONGVIEW FARM

Joanna Reed died in October 2002 at the age of eighty-five after gardening at Longview Farm for more than sixty years. The four-acre garden she created through her adult life in Malvern, Pennsylvania, has been noted and celebrated by garden writers including Rosemary Verey and Ellen Samuels in *The American Woman's Garden* (1984), where Joanna's own accounting can be read, and Starr Ockenga in *Earth on Her Hands: The American Woman in Her Garden* (1998). Joanna's son now lives in the Pennsylvania farmhouse where he was raised with his siblings, so Joanna's gardening passions and lessons live on in the next generation of gardeners. This includes her own children, several of whom are deeply involved in horticulture, as well as Michael Bowells, who lives and gardens next door on property Joanna sold him, and David Culp, who considered her a mentor and has followed in her footsteps by building a garden around an old Pennsylvania farmhouse and barn, celebrating that character.

In 1940, as newlyweds, Joanna and her husband, George, started their lives together on a property appearing less than ideal. The neglected farm and 1780 stone farmhouse with smoke-damaged rooms and failing sewage system nevertheless appealed to them because of its charm. Joanna had been trained as an artist at the Philadelphia School of Industrial Art (now the University of the Arts) and planned to paint at Longview. But a car broke down in front of their house and changed that plan. When Albert Barnes of the Barnes Foundation sought her help with his car, Joanna learned about the Laura Barnes Arboretum School in Merion, Pennsylvania, and she became one of the first students in the horticulture program there. Through that experience she became a plant collector; but even so, through all the decades of acquiring and planting hundreds of plants, many rarities, she never denied or jeopardized the charm and character of the Pennsylvania farm. Her garden is not a fancy garden; but it spoke and continues to speak to gardeners in the region, in part because of its appropriateness to place and expression of Pennsylvania character.

Capturing the sense of place

It's fair to say that all that remained when Joanna began gardening at Longview Farm was the essence or bones of the farm. The details were long gone due to neglect. Joanna preserved and accentuated the sense of place by honoring and building upon what remained. The farmhouse was restored in a way to keep

At Longview Farm the boundaries of the old fields, pastures, and livestock yard gave rise to the shape of the gardens and borders. The corncrib-turned-gazebo in the background, while brought to the site, builds on the farm character already established there and provides a sense of place.

Outbuildings left from the days when the property was an active farm now serve new uses and blend with the garden at Longview Farm, thereby preserving the character of the Pennsylvania farmhouse and region that first attracted the Reeds to the property.

its original character—whitewashed stucco and stone walls with cedar shingles. Functional shutters remain on the small paned windows. There are no screens (Joanna said insects could fly out just as easily as they flew in when the screenless windows were opened).

The dilapidated barn, propped up and painted red, became the place where garden equipment was stored. A small mowing tractor replaced the farm tractor. The basic rectilinear outline of the pastures persisted in the borders and stone walls Joanna added. Farm lanes and old cart roads evolved into garden pathways. A former pasture or field became a meadow. Because of this, the various farm outbuildings never appeared out of place or ill suited to their changing surroundings.

Borders, especially the one Joanna added after the Pennsylvania turnpike cut through the property in the 1940s, mimicked hedgerows. She planted native trees and shrubs, including sycamores, sour gums, eastern larches, and American arborvitae, and allowed red maples and ashes that self-sowed there to grow on. These were all well suited to the wet habitat that resulted from the highway construction. Perennials native to wet meadows added bold casual color: Joe Pye weed, ironweed, coneflower, and meadowsweet (respectively, *Eupatorium maculatum, Vernonia* spp., *Echinacea* spp., *Filipendula* spp.).

Deriving beauty from function

The farmhouse and barn provide two dominant focal points at Longview Farm. They provided essential shelter for the family and storage for garden equipment and tools, while they also set the personality of the place.

One of the first gardens Joanna developed was sensibly a vegetable garden to help feed the growing family, but she laid it out with an eye to design and historical precedents, not just with the harvest in mind. Inspired by the colonial four-square gardens at George Washington's birthplace—Wakefield—in Virginia, she staked out her eighty-by-eighty vegetable garden with axial pathways and a central modest dipping pool. Decades later when the vegetable garden's harvest was no longer needed to the same extent, vegetables gracefully gave way to ornamentals.

The stone walls, many built by Joanna herself or family members she enlisted to help, provided definition, enclosure, and a means to terrace slopes. Made of stone dug up on the property while planting beds were being prepared, these were laid dry and added beauty in and of themselves, again reminiscent of colonial practices. They also provided a constant in a dramatically changing deciduous eastern landscape. In one instance, a stone wall four and a half feet high added a sense of privacy and protection from intensifying traffic on the road in front of the house.

Off one corner of the barn, a cistern that once captured rainwater from the roof to water the livestock first served to corral young children like a playpen. It later became an ornamental pool graced with water lilies and frogs. The livestock yard became the Pool Garden.

The water lily pool Joanna created was first a cistern used to water livestock with rainwater collected off the barn. It then became a playpen for her young children before featuring water lilies.

The corncrib added to the site provides a gazebo in keeping with the farm's character.

Using humble materials

Keeping and recycling the original farmhouse and outbuildings is the most obvious example of Joanna's use of humble materials. Retaining the cedar shakes, wooden shutters, and whitewashed stone and stucco on the house, and the tin roof and board-and-batten siding on the barn, served to maintain a genuineness of character, lending the integrity of materials with historic ties to the site and humble personalities.

Split-rail fences, in addition to stone walls, provided enclosures sympathetic with the farm character and rural setting. For pathways, Joanna employed such recycled and local materials as crushed brick in one area, and flagstone from Avondale (a local quarry) in another area where it proved impossible to keep some well-traveled paths in turf. In the front garden, serving as an entry courtyard, she relied on crushed gravel—a material that could take the traffic around the house and yet create an appropriate ambiance.

Along the lanes or old cart roads, skeletons of abandoned farm equipment provided sculptural elements in the naturalistic plantings. Perhaps they also served as reminders that the sweeps of wildflowers and native plants under the trees were shaped by Joanna or the hand of woman, where one might otherwise think the woodland garden and meadow areas were the work of mother nature.

The inside and the outside are brought together by the simple balcony across the back of the farmhouse, where one can take in broad views of the garden.

For Joanna's eightieth birthday, her children gave her an old wire corncrib from some other farm. While it's separate from the other farm buildings, set up on a hill at the top of the pasture-turned-meadow, one would assume it has always been part of the farm. Instead of filling it with corn, she added a few garden chairs inside the cylindrical form, turning it into a garden gazebo. Its wire sides provided support for various clematis and other vines. It became a destination, even if one didn't take the time to sit and socialize there; it created a place and defined a space from which to take in an overview of the landscape.

Marrying the inside to the outside

On the front of the farmhouse a canopied open-air walkway provides a sense of entry and of protection from the outside. Entering the house there provides a chance to absorb the Front Garden. The gravel courtyard includes a small pool, containers, and ornamental plantings set off by the privacy stone wall that Joanna added between the house and the road. Despite the proximity of the road to the house, visitors entering the house are presented with an engaging view of this intimate and surprisingly tranquil garden composition.

On the back of the farmhouse, a balcony invites visitors outside for an overview of the ornamental formal herb garden below, the expanse of meadow, and the surrounding woods and borders beyond. Close to the kitchen, the balcony also provided a place to dine outside. Thus, both the front and back façades of the house create a strong connection to the outside, a connection preserved without punching into the historical house to add modern glass doors or windows.

Joanna was also well known for her crewel embroidery. She captured the plants in her garden in lifelike embroidered curtains hung in the living room, thus bringing the outdoors inside. These botanical paintings in yarn have been featured in magazines such as *Fine Threads*.

Involving the visitor

By developing garden spaces with distinct personalities based on the lay of the farmland, such as the Front Garden, the Pool Garden, and the Vegetable Garden with its herb parterre, Joanna provided visitors to Longview Farm with the experience of a stroll garden and a sequence of discovery as they followed paths and lanes from one space to another. The balcony provided a broad overview, while the pockets and enclosed gardens tucked between outbuildings and the sculptural focal points such as benches and artfully abandoned farm machinery provided moments of discovery and engagement.

Joanna was also famous for her passion for herbs. An active member of the American Herb Society, she engaged the senses of smell and taste directly in her garden by having visitors crush and sniff herbs while walking through and then feeding them lunches seasoned with herbs from the garden. It was hard for visitors to leave her garden without feeling a direct connection to it.

ASHLAND HOLLOW

William and Nancy Frederick both grew up in northern Delaware and met in college, when Bill studied at Swarthmore (and interned at the Scott Arboretum) and Nancy attended Bryn Mawr nearby. After their marriage and law school, Bill decided to forsake law to pursue his passion for plants and design. They returned to northern Delaware and established a nursery, and they also began raising a family and building a home in the rolling Piedmont Hills north of Wilmington, near the Pennsylvania border and within spitting distance of the renowned Winterthur and Longwood Gardens, both of which had great influence on Bill (he retired from the Board of Longwood in 2007 after serving 36 years). Later he practiced landscape architecture, specializing in residential gardens.

Planning for their property started in 1963 with the design of the house, a low-slung, sprawling stucco structure built spanning a natural stream valley. The house was completed in 1965 and attention turned to the development of the garden, which has been added to methodically over the course of three decades based on the original master plan. A journey through the garden leads up the stream valley above the house and back, passing through areas known as the Entrance Garden, the Stream Valley Garden, the Studio Garden, the Persimmon Grove, the Game Lawn, the Swimming Pool Garden, the Vegetable Garden, the Winter Garden, the Hillside Meadow, the Dark Green, White, and Gray Path, the Shrub Rose Path, the Wisteria Walk, and the Frog Steps.

The Fredericks' garden is probably bigger than any garden most of us will ever undertake, but these principles work in multi-acre gardens as well as postage-stamp-sized ones. Bill, a consummate plantsman, has authored several books offering detailed knowledge and observations about plants and design. His *100 Great Garden Plants* was originally published in 1975 and reprinted by Timber Press in 1986 and *The Exuberant Garden and the Controlling Hand* followed in 1992. While novice gardeners may be intimidated by Bill's background, whether we're learning to swim, play the clarinet, or make a garden, don't we want to learn from masters and accomplished performers?

Capturing the sense of place

The development of Ashland Hollow focused on the stream running through the valley or "hollow." The design of the house and garden responds to and celebrates the beauty of the stream. This is expressed most dramatically by the fact that the

The house at Ashland Hollow bridges the stream on the property.

house straddles the stream. Water flows through architectural arches directly beneath an expansive living-dining room. In this airy room, artwork covers one wall but two other walls are punctuated by numerous window-doors that frame views up and down the stream valley. It would be hard not to notice the state of the stream on a daily basis living at Ashland Hollow, given the intimacy with the stream that the architecture fosters. The window-doors on the west side of the living room allow guests and dwellers to step outside onto a balcony above the stream, making the connections between indoor activities and the outside even closer.

This view up the stream valley from the balcony of the house is part of the everyday experience of living at Ashland Hollow.

The house isn't visible as you enter the driveway from the country road. Tucked low in the valley, nestled among the native tulip and beech trees, it remains hidden until the drive circles through a wooded section and drops down into the entrance courtyard. The fact that the eastern deciduous woods envelop the house emphasizes the natural landscape or character of the place.

Making the stream the heart of the garden has led to distinct and memorable garden areas. The journey upstream to the spring reveals a series of spaces dominated by water. In a broad section of the stream just above the house, a man-made pyramidal island covered with selaginella is the focal point; farther upstream a small waterfall composed of both natural and carved stones creates a space enlivened with the sights and sounds of falling water (a photograph of this water feature appears in the first chapter); and finally, a still pool edged with marsh marigold (*Caltha palustris*) and surrounded by Japanese umbrella pines (*Sciadopitys verticillata*) creates a quiet retreat where the water wells up and gives birth to the stream.

Deriving beauty from function

The Fredericks' house has no gutters. Instead, rain falls from the eaves onto large river rocks set in a band along the base of the house. A channel beneath the rocks then carries the rainwater away from the foundation. When wet from rain, the stones glisten, adding a natural dynamic beauty not found with conventional gutters. This approach first allows the rain to be observed and then turns it into a serendipitous water feature. The smooth, round shapes and earthy colors of the river rocks provide a connection to the rocks and colors of nature found in the garden.

The long entry drive carefully skirts the stream valley and ultimately leads to the front door, where it broadens into a courtyard surrounded on three sides by the house and garages. In its design, the driveway was integrated with the house so that the experience of arrival is both a visually pleasing and a physically easy experience. The entry court functions as part of the driveway and is on the same grade as the entry walk to the house. The stone "gutters" contribute to the garden aspect of the courtyard.

The Swimming Pool Garden is very much a garden, even though it's also a pool well suited for swimming. The required fence enclosing the pool is of a black chain link, but it essentially disappears since it runs through a wide bed of maroon-leaved barberry (*Berberis thunbergii* 'Crimson Pygmy') planted on the hill sloping down to the pool. Oval in shape, the pool is surrounded by a random stone terrace, broken by patches of perennials planted in irregular pockets. Fountains of ornamental grasses and dramatic verbascums soften the stone edge of the pool, taking a cue from how cattails or skunk cabbage soften the edges of wet areas in the region with their fine and bold-textured leaves.

The walls of the pool are gray, making the water appear more like a natural pond than if they had been painted white as pool walls typically are. A structure that looks like a small barn adjoining the terrace houses the necessary pool machinery and equipment. It predates the pool and perhaps at one time served as a springhouse or mill house. A grape-covered arbor added off the pool house partially covers the terrace, providing shade near the pool. While obviously man-made, the Swimming Pool Garden captures some of the feel of a fishing pond and boathouse. Whether you have a bathing suit or not, it's a pleasure to view and be in and it fits with the rural character of the site.

A stone springhouse or mill house on the property now houses the pool equipment, while a rustic grape arbor of cedar logs provides a canopy of shade next to the pool.

The oval swimming pool is an abstraction of a pond, with planting spaces in the terrace allowing ornamental grasses, verbascums, and other perennials to soften the edge. The requisite enclosing fence is hidden in the bed of maroon-leaved barberry and doesn't take away from the beauty of the scene.

Not far from the kitchen, a dinner bell sits on top of a cedar trunk, providing a way to signal when it's time to come in from the garden for a meal. With the kids grown, it may not be used much nowadays, but even when silent it adds a sculptural element to the landscape and blends with the woods with its nicely weathered post of eastern red cedar.

Using humble materials

The use of a rustic cedar log to support the dinner bell is also an example of using a humble material. It's conceivable that the post was made from the trunk of a native eastern red cedar (*Juniperus virginiana*) grown on the property that got shaded out as the surrounding woods matured.

Besides a springhouse or mill house being recycled into the pool house, a farm barn on the upper edge of the stream valley was also adaptively reused to provide an office for Bill's landscape architecture practice. The character of the barn was honored; it still looks like part of a traditional Pennsylvania farm, so views to it from the garden don't detract from the beauty and rural feel of that section of the garden. The path climbs a slope from the Winter Garden that passes through the Hillside Meadow, a naturalistic blend of goldenrods, asters, and native grasses with

The trunk of an old cedar holds the dinner bell, an object that served to call in family members as well as add ornamentation to the garden.

Recycled railroad ties form the steps leading up to the barn-turned-office. The yews planted on the meadow hillside emulate the eastern red cedars (*Juniperus virginiana*) that frequently grow in abandoned farm fields.

a few yews interspersed to imitate eastern red cedars seeding into old fields. At the top of the path, the view stops with the red barn-turned-office. Its outward appearance is in keeping with the Hillside Meadow, even though office equipment has replaced farm tools inside. The steps of the path are formed from true old railroad ties, another example of a humble and recycled material.

Even with its sprawling footprint, the house blends sympathetically with the surrounding woods, in part due to its tan stucco finish, the color of dried leaves, and in part due to its dark brown roof tiles that emulate cedar shingles while being made of a synthetic fireproof material. The river rocks used in the rain channels anchoring the foundation to the landscape also count again here as modest building materials that blend with the garden.

Marrying the inside to the outside

The house is married to the site at Ashland Hollow in numerous and varied ways. Its distinct design, like that of Fallingwater, was dictated by the site. It couldn't be duplicated on the "lot next door." The multiple window-doors in the living room provide ample opportunity to look up and down the stream valley and to step outside directly from the heart of the house.

A separate building serving as a studio lies in the garden on the opposite side of the stream from the front entrance. It's surrounded by a brick-paved terrace that's broken up with planting beds. Moving from the house to the studio requires taking a short garden walk. The terrace beds are planted for multiseasonal and architectural interest, with topiaries and bright patches of tulips in the spring and vivid annuals in the summer. From inside the studio, windows with peaked frames offer uniquely outlined garden vignettes distinct from the stream valley views offered by the main house.

Back at the main house, the outside is carried inside in a whimsical way. The entrance hallway there is painted with a trompe l'oeil of a neglected formal garden where native plants such as trumpet vine (*Campsis radicans*) overtake classical statuary.

The portion of the house spanning the stream mimics the lines of a curved garden bridge with its arched curtain walls. In this open-air chamber beneath the living room, the stream flows through a rock-lined channel that's narrow enough to step over. Suspended across the channel here is a hammock, fastened to opposite corners of the room. Seeking shade there on a hot summer day, one feels the cooling effects of the water while swaying in the hammock, no doubt a magical blend of inside comforts and outside experiences.

Despite all the windows, doors, and terrace areas already connecting the house to the outside, the Fredericks modified the casual eating area in the kitchen by adding a large bay window. This allows them to take in views of the stream valley and also enjoy an indoor display of forced bulbs and other potted plants on the windowsill while eating simple meals there.

The first room of the house, a garden room with exposed rafters, features fragrant plants and assures that visitors to the property have a garden experience even after stepping through the "front door."

The driveway flowing into an entry courtyard circled by the house brings the outside and the inside together gracefully. Once a guest approaches the front door, the tie between the architecture of the house and the outside is further reinforced by the Entrance Garden, a garden room tucked under the roofline of the house. A trellis frames a doorway in line with the outside wall of the house and a few rafters continue the roofline although a sweet bay magnolia (*Magnolia virginiana*) planted in the room pokes up above the rafters. Native azaleas and woody plants espaliered on the walls and a bowl-shaped fountain offering a single jet of water complete the furnishings in this entry room.

Involving the visitor

Ashland Hollow was designed as a stroll garden. The orchestrated walk through the garden starts at the house and leads up the stream valley on one side and then circles back to the house on the other to reveal a sequence of experiences as rich as that offered by any Japanese or Chinese stroll garden. Areas have distinct functions, in the case of the vegetable garden, the play area, and the nursery areas for growing plants for the garden, or have distinct design goals—an area for winter interest, a wisteria display, a path lined with exuberant shrub roses offering winter, spring, and summer bloom interest—making the journey rewarding and never repetitious regardless of the season.

Landscape elements found along the way involve the garden traveler in specific activities. There are the doors into the Winter Garden and the Hillside Meadow, causing guests to climb a few steps, open a traditional house door, and pass through a door frame, emphasizing the transition from one space to another. At another point on the path, a gazebo on stilts challenges all to climb its few steps for a perfect bird's-eye view down the Dark Green, White, and Gray Path.

At the end of this path, off to one side and hidden from view by dogwoods, sits the huge sculptural frog described and pictured in the previous chapter. This fiberglass work of art, more than six feet wide and nine feet tall, pays tribute to all the frogs living in Ashland Hollow. Bill invites guests to turn the frog into a prince; those who oblige by kissing the frog are rewarded with a loud croak controlled and perfectly timed by either Bill or Nancy—a humorous and surprising way to engage visitors in the garden.

Recall the Entrance Garden? The sound and movement of the jet of water in the small fountain by the front door, plus the fragrance from the long-blooming magnolia and the native azaleas planted in this outdoor room, confront and engage multiple senses in the short time required to pass from the car through the courtyard to the front door. So even if guests arrive and don't later venture out into the garden, they've been briefly engaged in the garden in this one intense space.

LA CASITA DE MARIA

When Jan and Bill Frieder moved from Michigan to Arizona (so Bill could coach basketball for Arizona State University), Jan wanted to find a home that would be characteristic of the new and distinctly different environment they would be living in—in the language of this book, one that would reflect a sense of place. When she found La Casita de Maria, a modest adobe dwelling built in the 1920s, she found what she was looking for. Though in need of repair and now surrounded by the sprawling subdevelopments of Phoenix, the Paradise Valley property had charm and original character, so the Frieders purchased it in 1989. The focus of the courtyard, bas-relief tiles depicting the Virgin Mary, gave rise to the name of the property, which means "the little house of Mary." Jan, with encouragement from Bill, began working with designers, including landscape architect Christie Ten Eyck, to bring new life to the property while respecting, honoring, and drawing inspiration from its humble history.

The original house had two bedrooms, while a second separate building contained a garage and a small apartment, and a third building consisted of two small guest quarters. All exhibited classic Arizona style with their small scale, simple adobe walls, boxy lines, flat roofs, and few embellishments. Adding a master bedroom and swimming pool without destroying the sense of scale nor the outdoor courtyard spaces was just one of the challenges in the renovation and updating process. Along the way, the old garage was converted into a den, and a new garage was added, taking on the persona of a horse barn. The garden and courtyard spaces were to retain the feel of an "old farm lady's garden."

Capturing the sense of place

Inside, the sense of place and history was preserved through such efforts as keeping the original bathroom fixtures, finding additional old fixtures instead of buying new ones, and re-enameling them. New chrome plumbing fixtures were subjected to acid and steel wool to dull their shine. Outside, preservation involved keeping but moving the enclosing adobe wall and gateway entrance in order to accommodate the additions to the house.

The temptation to remove walls or add large rooms with modern-day dimensions was carefully avoided in order to preserve the small, intimate scale of the 1920s cottage-style architecture. New materials were carefully modeled on existing materials: old concrete windowsills were salvaged and new ones were

Mesquite, desert willow, cactus, and native wildflowers surrounding the three separate buildings forming the Frieder residence impart an unmistakable sense of place.

made with the same thickness and angle. Concrete floors in new additions were matched to the old; outside, new concrete paving poured in the central courtyard was troweled so it would fit the spirit of the site.

The garden plants existing at the beginning of the renovation such as prickly pear cactus and creosote bushes were preserved and complemented with mature desert trees such as palo verde (*Cercidium floridum*), desert willow (*Chilopsis linearis*), and native mesquite (*Prosopis* spp.), reflecting the desert flora that would have been prevalent in the surrounding Sonoran desert before the casita was surrounded with development. A single picture of this property provides many clues as to what part of the country it's in. La Casita de Maria captures the essence of its place, inside and out.

Deriving beauty from function

The house consisting of three separate buildings is the dominant landscape feature, but with its earth-colored adobe walls blending with the gravel pathways and the concrete-paved courtyard, it doesn't overwhelm the site. The walls provide backdrops to colorful annuals and desert wildflowers tucked into pockets and planting spaces to conserve water. Shadows cast from the courtyard trees seem to create constantly changing artwork on the many exterior walls. In the original design of the dwelling, the water well was disguised as an *horno*, a traditional Pueblo Indian outdoor oven, thereby adding beauty and interest to the landscape while reflecting local traditions.

To blend with the rounded door and window frames and the rounded corners of the adobe buildings, the swimming pool was designed with rounded corners—so while modern, its personality draws from the traditional architectural character. The gray-green plaster and green slate tiles lining the pool help to further blend it with the landscape, and a border around the pool only two feet wide allows the desert vegetation to embrace the pool, spill over its edges, and have the plants' distinctive forms reflected in the water. To enclose the pool, a traditional ocotillo fence (made of prickly stems from *Fouquieria splendens* tied side by side) was used instead of a modern manufactured one. So while well suited to swimming laps, the pool also helps capture the essence of the place.

Using humble materials

The entrance to the property, a gravel lane with poorly defined edges due to naturalistic plantings along either side, leads up to a gate creating an opening in the adobe wall. It retains the feel of a country lane; there's no sign of expensive paving or edging materials here to make a first impression. A fine gravel or grit is also used for paths off the central concrete courtyard.

Adobe, the primary building material used in the buildings and garden walls, symbolizes the Southwest and its history. Made from the earth itself, with straw thrown in to bind it together, it couldn't be any humbler or more closely linked to the place. The adobe is suitably complemented with other humble materials: concrete floors both inside and out, wood ceilings, rustic vigas (logs forming the roofs and extending out from the adobe walls), and untreated copper drainpipes.

An original window in the house made from a stack of bottles laid on their sides allows light to come in while preserving privacy. The window is, in a sense, a folk art imitation of stained glass using recycled objects. From the outside, the circular glass bottoms of the bottles embedded in the adobe repeat the shape of circular flowerpots nearby and the colors found in the garden.

Mature trees brought to the site to replace weedy introduced tamarisk trees and provide shade were salvaged from a canal expansion project occurring a short distance from the house. Garden furniture added to the central courtyard has the lines of 1920s overstuffed living room furniture, although it's made of twigs so it feels like it belongs in the outdoor room.

The original 1920s design for La Casita de Maria included this *horno*, an outside oven in the style and form of the traditional Pueblo Indian ovens, although in this case it was added to disguise the water well.

The lap pool, although a 1990s addition, blends with the original character of the property by borrowing rounded corners from the doorways and windows of the house and by borrowing colors from the desert. The cactus and desert wildflowers spilling over the narrow edge of the pool soften its outline; their images reflected in the water intensify the beauty of the garden.

The understated entrance to the property is as it was in the 1920s although it had to be moved and rebuilt in order to accommodate the additions to the house.

The outside can easily be enjoyed by visitors staying in the guest rooms. With one step they can go from their bedroom to a private terrace and enjoy native Arizona plants in the garden landscape.

Marrying the inside to the outside

An opening in the adobe wall enclosing the central courtyard serves as an entry gateway. A massive beam over the gate prominently displays the name of the house in faded paint. This doorway has the feel of a front door, so that stepping through the opening is like entering a room, although outdoors. The central courtyard is strongly defined by the garden wall and the three buildings, so that it truly feels like a room of the house.

Living in this house with its separate structures means passing through the central courtyard or garden space, which functions as a hallway or foyer, on a daily basis. Even from inside the one-story house, with so many external walls, doors, and windows, nearly every room has several direct links to the garden outside. And once the light of the day has faded, sounds from the garden still penetrate indoors due to the small gurgling fountain in the center of the courtyard. Lying in bed, the occupants can be lulled to sleep by these sounds.

Views of the desert and the mountains beyond the garden perimeter involve visitors in a broader landscape.

A small terrace added to the guest rooms means guests can access the outside in a single step without appearing in the more public central courtyard. They can privately enjoy the connection to outdoor garden spaces from their rooms.

Involving the visitor

A sense of mystery (and privacy) is created by the adobe wall and buildings surrounding the internal courtyard. Visitors are pulled into the space through the narrow opening—the gateway—to discover what's at its heart. The small ornamental water fountain consisting of a stone basin and gravel-lined catch basin, pictured in the previous chapter, creates the heartbeat and engages the visitor through sight and sound with its animated dance of water. From inside this sanctuary, what lies outside the walls feels remote. Furthermore, the distinct buildings create corners and hidden pockets to discover, whether these spaces shelter a *horno* or a shrine devoted to Mary.

Another modern addition, an outdoor stairway that borrows from ancient pueblo design, invites visitors to climb to a rooftop deck. From there, broader views of the garden, the surrounding landscape, and the dramatic mountains in the distance lead to a greater awareness of and involvement with the setting.

The courtyard features a mystery waiting to be discovered, an alcove with bas-relief tiles depicting the Virgin Mary, for whom the property was named.

THE BRANDYWINE CONSERVANCY
RIVER MUSEUM

Although best known for the collection of paintings by Wyeth family members housed in its museum, the Brandywine Conservancy's mission is to preserve the natural, historic, and cultural heritage of the Brandywine River country. The conservancy aims to recognize what's special about the region that inspired the Brandywine Painters School and keep it intact. Through impressive land planning as well as conservation and private partnership efforts, the Brandywine Conservancy has succeeded in preserving open space and managing development so that the Brandywine River Valley is still full of scenic drives. When the conservancy purchased the museum site in Chadds Ford, Pennsylvania, in 1967 to prevent the development of an industrial park on the banks of the river, it had been the site of a lumber supply company. Troubled by periodic flooding of the lumber storage yard, the lumber company had tried filling the area with coal cinders and other rubble before giving up and selling the property. Ultimately the nineteenth-century gristmill building came to house the art collection, and the lumberyard became the museum's parking lot and gardens. At first, plants such as exotic cotoneasters filled the role of foundation plantings, but when FM Mooberry, a volunteer during the garden's early days, became coordinator of horticulture, the landscape around the museum began to "walk the talk" of the organization. A new approach to the museum grounds developed, one that said something about the Brandywine Valley and expressed the mission of the institution.

The gardens, essentially composed of the beds in the parking lot and in the area around the museum buildings, have been maintained largely by a corps of volunteers who carry on the work FM Mooberry started, although she retired more than fifteen years ago. The ultimate compliment from visitors that FM liked to hear was "The gardens look so natural we thought they were just there"—words that proved that the natural character of the region had been reestablished on top of a coal cinder field and former lumberyard.

Capturing the sense of place

The palette of plants used in the gardens at the Brandywine River Museum celebrates the vegetative and visual character of the valley. Sweeps of daylilies, though not a native plant, emulate the ubiquitous presence of daylilies along Pennsylvania

This former mill building now serves as the Brandywine River Museum. The closed wooden shutters preserve the original architecture of the building while providing an appropriately protective environment for the art collection housed within.

country roads in the region; native plants found in floodplains or growing along roadsides or at the edges of pastures and farmland fill the planting beds—Joe Pye weed, aster, and goldenrod, along with trees and shrubs such as river birch, swamp cypress, and winterberry hollies that can tolerate the extremes of wet and dry that come with the periodic flooding of the site.

While the landscape outside conveys the sense of the Brandywine Valley, much of the artwork inside, by members of the Wyeth family and other regional artists, contains images of Pennsylvania farmhouses, barns, livestock, landscapes, and people. By capturing the sense of place on canvas, these artists have brought international awareness to some of the unique aspects of the Brandywine Valley.

Deriving beauty from function

The gardens function as the parking lot, or vice versa. Visitors to the Brandywine River Museum park between the naturalistically planted garden beds. Roughly half the parking lot isn't paved with a hard surface; there parking places appear as a green expanse between raised island beds that are full of wildflowers and defined by "curbs" of recycled railroad ties. From Route 1, the first view of the museum is across the wildflower plantings, making the introduction to the site very different from a view across a sea of asphalt.

The storm water retention basin, set in one of the parking lot islands, resembles a bog or small pond more than a conventional overflow storage basin. Yellow flag iris and cattails grow in the pool, swamp cypress and winterberry holly around it. If you crop out the surrounding cars from the view by looking through your hands like a camera viewfinder, you might think you were in the New Jersey Pine Barrens instead of the middle of a museum parking lot.

Other necessary visitor amenities celebrate the historical character of the site. Trash cans have been made from large old wooden barrels; lampposts in the parking lot are made of rough-cut lumber (perhaps a reference to the lumberyard days) and double as supports for native vines such as trumpet creeper (*Campsis radicans*).

An old wooden barrel serving as a trash can doesn't detract from the aesthetics of the site.

Bollards, used to keep cars from galloping across the wide pedestrian walkways, are recycled hitching posts, complete with ornamental horse heads and rings for tying reins to.

A split-rail fence defines and protects the parking lot and property in keeping with the traditional signature style of fencing in the region. Near the entrance to the museum building itself, the circular foundation of a large silo left from when the building functioned as a gristmill now serves as a pleasing pedestal to display a large piece of sculpture. The feature fits so gracefully in the landscape, it's easy to assume the base was built for that purpose.

Using humble materials

The numerous instances of recycling on the site serve as examples of using humble materials: the mill building converted into the museum; the lumber storage yard becoming the parking lot; the Victorian house next door becoming the office building for the conservancy's land management staff. The loading dock of the mill was readily converted into an entry courtyard and an appropriate means to "load" visitors into the museum. To appropriately protect the artwork, windows were sealed off and the wooden shutters on the outside were closed, thus preserving the appearance of the building's façade and the vernacular architectural style.

In addition, old grinding millstones have been converted to serve various purposes: as ornamental paving stones in walkways, as stepping-stones, and as benches and tables on the side of the museum facing the river, where a trail invites visitors to explore the banks and watch the water flow. Recycled cobblestones pave the entry courtyard and outline the path edges; old city curbstones stacked several high form a protective knee-high wall along the edge of the property where it meets Route 1.

New materials with modest personalities introduced to the site include an aggregate river stone paving material for walkways. Although washed by some other river, the paving material makes the walkways look like loose gravel even though they're stable, with the small river stones embedded in a concrete mixture. The appearance is in keeping with the character of the gardens and buildings, while the material provides the same ease of use that plain concrete or asphalt would. The rough-cut lumber lampposts, the split-rail fencing, and the gravel used to cover the river path and parking lot, although newly added, feel regionally connected and sympathetic to the rural, pastoral character being celebrated.

Marrying the inside to the outside

Most museums have little connection to the outside due to the critically important need to protect the objects inside; however, at the Brandywine River Museum, the outside has been dramatically brought inside with the addition of a rounded glass tower that provides corridors to connect art galleries in the old section of the former mill to those in the new section of the museum. As visitors pass from one

The use of recycled city curbstones along the split-rail fence exemplifies the principle of relying on humble or regionally appropriate material, as does the use of crushed gravel and railroad ties in the parking lot.

Recycled millstones serve as benches, tables, and paving pieces.

A circular glass-walled tower brings the inside and the outside together. To visitors passing through the glass corridors between art galleries, spectacular views of the Brandywine River appear as living art.

Visitors become engaged in the site by following the trail by the museum that allows them to observe the river close at hand.

gallery to another on all levels of the museum, they take in panoramic views of the Brandywine River, the site's most dramatic and dynamic feature. The wall of the museum's café next to the river is also largely glass, allowing visitors to observe the landscape while they dine, thus connecting them to the outside.

Pieces of the art collection that include scenes of the countryside also capture the outside inside the galleries.

Involving the visitor

Because wildflower plantings intermingle with the parking lot, visitors are engaged with the unconventional gardens of the Brandywine River Museum before they step out of their cars. While few come just to visit the gardens or appreciate the outdoors, I imagine most end up doing both, since they see the river and the pathway along its banks while walking through the glass-walled connecting corridors between galleries. The view teases them to experience the river up close, and the stroll path that allows them to do so guides them along the bank of the river to discover additional sculptural pieces, the benches and picnic tables made from giant millstones, and scenic vistas of the river.

The Crosby Arboretum in Picayune, Mississippi, a young garden in the field of public gardens, opened to the public in 1984 after several years of development. Unlike traditional gardens designed for public enjoyment and education, with collections of plants from around the world, the Crosby Arboretum is a collection of natural areas chosen to preserve unique types of forests and habitats. One site serves as a 104-acre interpretive center and introduction to the seven natural areas comprising nearly 1000 acres of the Pearl River Basin. The Crosby Arboretum is an acknowledgment that to preserve natural areas, humans may need to intercede in some ways—for instance, by culling exotic weeds or introducing fire in pieces of habitat that depend on a fire-based ecology.

The arboretum was conceived of as a living memorial to L. O. Crosby, Jr., a southern Mississippi timber pioneer and philanthropist, who died in 1978. The first director, landscape architect Ed Blake, befuddled local residents with his visionary idea of an arboretum, while at the same time he was lauded by native plant lovers for recognizing that the bogs and savannas and forests of Mississippi shouldn't be taken for granted. The interpretation and education provided by the arboretum would ensure that their profound beauty, richness, and importance were more fully appreciated.

Capturing the sense of place

The mission of this institution is to recognize the unique habitats found in the Pearl River Basin and to preserve those habitats, so capturing the essence of nature in the region is the focus and reason for being for this organization, much like the Brandywine Conservancy. The natural areas in the network were acquired with the diversity of the flora and the beauty of the sites in mind. In the various distinct habitats being preserved as part of the Crosby Arboretum network, ranging from hillside bogs to beech-magnolia forests, more than three hundred species of trees, shrubs, wildflowers, and grasses native to south-central Mississippi and southeast Louisiana can be found.

The naturalistic interpretive center serves as an introduction to the various natural areas. It appears to be a natural area as well, but it required planting and tending and management in order to portray the various habitats found in the disjointed network of natural areas. The beauty of the piney woods inspired architect Fay Jones with the design for the main structure to serve visitors on the site,

Pinecote Pavilion at the Crosby Arboretum in Picayune, Mississippi, captures the character of the piney woods in its architecture; its reflection in the lake ties it intimately to the arboretum.

The support posts in Pinecote Pavilion branch at their tops in imitation of the pines surrounding the structure.

The roof of Pinecote Pavilion gradually gives way to the garden; its pattern draws from the patterns created by needles and branches.

Pinecote Pavilion, completed in 1987. The numerous tall, closely spaced supports for the A-frame roof of the pavilion resemble the trunks of the pines ringing it. The posts branch near their tops like the pines to support the rafters. The roof, sheathed in cedar shingles, gives way to trelliswork and exposed rafters at the edge of the pavilion, creating a canopy that mimics the patterns created by the branches and the needles of the pines. As described by Robert Adams Ivy, Jr., in his 1992 book about the architect: "Clearly a built object, this simple shed responds to its setting so strongly that comparisons of building to nature seem inevitable" (76). It manifests the essence of the piney woods in architecture. Fay Jones even referred to it as "an abstract forest."

Deriving beauty from function

Pinecote Pavilion is a work of architectural art (having won the American Institute of Architects—or AIA—Honor Award in 1990, the National Design Award from the American Wood Council in 1987, and the First Award from the Red Cedar Shingle and Hand-Split Shake Bureau with AIA in 1987) that provides shelter and creates a gathering place for programs and events. It's a man-made sculpture that provides a reference or focal point as visitors venture off on trails, over bridges and boardwalks, through bogs, meadows, and woods. Regardless of the angle, the light, or the season, it's beautiful to look at.

Other smaller additions to the landscape serve equally important functions and also double as sculpture or points of beauty and interest because of their thoughtful design and execution. The drinking fountain, made of a stone pedestal with water jets at either end, resembles a pre-Hispanic ruin or artifact. Set in an open area for visitors to easily find and see to drink from, the fountain is attractive enough so that there's no need to hide it in an alcove or a shelter by bathrooms like a conventional drinking fountain. This one works as a fountain for both the eyes and the mouth to drink from.

Bridges and boardwalks at Pinecote provide the means to navigate the wetlands. Several broad bridges have sloping wooden benches on both sides that function as barrier railings and resting places. The weathered silvery boards of the bridges provide visual continuity as they blend with the color of the gravel pathway on either end of the bridges.

Similarly, canopied bulletin boards and trash cans of silvery weathered wood were designed to add to the beauty and architectural unity of the site. They weren't added as afterthoughts but rather seen as landscape or garden features that should be designed with the same thought and sensitivity to the site as the main pavilion.

Visitor amenities at the Crosby Arboretum were all treated as opportunities to add beauty and interest to the site. This drinking fountain doubles as a water feature; the water is captured underground for reuse in the garden.

Trash cans were specially designed to blend with the architecture and not detract from the natural beauty of the site.

The Crosby Arboretum features the humble native plants of the region and celebrates the unique landscape characteristics of this part of the country.

Using humble materials

The native plants of the bog and piney woods of Mississippi amounted to weeds in the estimation of some of the local residents when the Crosby Arboretum was first established. The native flora was regarded as so insignificant that the efforts being taken to preserve it were dubbed a folly. Now, perhaps because the focus of this "garden" is on the local flora, residents have a greater awareness and appreciation of those humble plants. With the loss of wetlands and bogs throughout much of the southeastern part of the country, we are slowly realizing the need to protect these fragile ecosystems and the "weeds" they provide home to.

Many of the paths that lead visitors on meandering journeys of discovery are no more than sandy trails. The humble personality of these helps create a sense that little human disturbance or intervention has gone on here. The paths blend with the sandy edges of bogs and the sandy soil of the piney woods. Further, the fact that the wood and shingles used in the bridges and Pinecote Pavilion are allowed to weather naturally helps to create a sense of *wabi-sabi* in the arboretum.

Visitors have multiple opportunities to come close to the lake while crossing small footbridges.

Marrying the inside to the outside

Standing in Pinecote Pavilion is simultaneously an indoor and an outdoor experience. While standing under the sheltering A-frame structure, visitors are still in the outside air and seemingly surrounded by pine trunks because of the way the support columns and the branching trusses seem to bring the pines into the interior of the structure.

The central aisle of Pinecote, clear of support posts, serves as a window to the pond and the landscape beyond. As visitors go inside, their view remains sharply focused on the outside by the frame created by the support posts outlining the central aisle. The pavilion is cantilevered over Gum Pond, which means visitors are suspended over water while inside. The pond water laps at the edge of the decklike platform in what feels like the nave of this awe-inspiring building, bringing visitors into sharp and intimate relationship with the pond and the water.

The pavilion is also accentuated by its reflection in the 2.5-acre lake. When viewed from the opposite side of the lake, the building creates a geometrical composition with the water. At night, the lights in the pavilion illuminate the ceiling and reflect in the lake, creating an image that looks like a sparkling cut gemstone surrounded by dark sky and water.

Involving the visitor

The Crosby Arboretum was designed as a stroll garden to enable visitors to discover distinct habitats and plant associations. At Pinecote, trails circle the pond, passing through woodland and wetland and revealing longleaf pines here, pitcher plants there, or views of Pinecote and vistas of savanna. Plants comfortably spill over the soft edges of the sandy paths in naturalistic style, meaning they're close enough for visitors to touch or smell. The pavilion pulls the visitor in and then reveals a panoramic view of the pond while not laying the paths bare; with such a dramatic entry experience, who wouldn't be drawn into the garden and want to explore what lies beyond?

Many of the trails disappear around bends into woods, creating that sense of mystery that pulls visitors into or engages them in the landscape. Literature from the arboretum refers to these trails as "path journeys"—indicating a form of engagement beyond just traveling over the ground. Indeed, to tour the seven natural areas in the arboretum, visitors must make pilgrimages and allocate the time needed to traverse the region, an experience that might engage them for days or a lifetime.

THE LADY BIRD JOHNSON
WILDFLOWER CENTER

The Lady Bird Johnson Wildflower Center, established in 1982, opened a public garden in southwest Austin, Texas, in 1995, with intent similar to that of the Crosby Arboretum. The garden, today a total of 279 acres, and the national programs conducted by the center were designed around and are governed by these principles:

> We honor and respect the natural beauty and biological heritage of each region of the country.
>
> We commit ourselves to conserving and restoring wildflowers, native plants, and the biological communities on which they depend.
>
> We encourage native flora through artful, naturalistic plantings in public, private, urban, and suburban landscapes.
>
> We use native plantings with regionally appropriate architecture to integrate the human community into the natural world in a responsible and respectful manner.
>
> We recognize that the health and well-being of human communities is directly related to the health of the land which sustains human life.

The center includes a series of designed landscapes and gardens at the core of the property along with a variety of facilities to serve visitors as well as educational and research purposes. Managed and restored meadow, savanna, and woodland areas typical of the Texas Hill Country ring the core area of the property.

Capturing the sense of place

While the center strives to show how native plants can be used in all styles of landscaping, from naturalistic to formal, a number of its gardens celebrate distinct naturally occurring plant communities and habitats of the Texas Hill Country, capturing the unique aspects of landscapes in that part of Texas. A shady entrance area features live oaks (*Quercus viriginiana*), while the Meadows shows central Texas wildflowers. Other garden areas feature prairie grasses and aquatic habitat. All are attempts to capture the essence of nature as it's manifested in Texas.

Walking trails lead visitors farther into the property, allowing them to discover rock outcroppings, a limestone cave, picturesque old oaks, architectural cactus, and expanses of savanna being restored to their original character. Visitors can thus form a sense of what the area was like before settlement and development.

Deriving beauty from function

Each building added to the center to provide visitor services or research support was treated as an opportunity to add a cultural or historical reflection of the region to the site. The large auditorium not only accommodates hundreds of participants for educational programs but also provides, with its massive stone walls, an attractive backdrop to the gardens and natural areas surrounding it. While the dark sandstone and ironwork of the auditorium reflect the Spanish influence and style of seventeenth-century missions, the light-colored limestone and straightforward outline of other buildings mark the German influence, and the barnlike farm buildings featuring galvanized metal and tin roofs capture the Texas ranch influence on the region's vernacular architecture. Rick Archer, architect and principal of Overland Partners Architects in San Antonio, was given the directive to reflect the special nature of Austin architecturally, while those involved in the organization set about capturing and preserving its special natural history in the gardens and restored natural areas.

The center is the first pre-existing site to be considered for LEED (Leadership in Energy and Environmental Design) certification. The harvesting of rainwater to use for irrigation created an opportunity to add ornamental water features—such as a raised aqueduct, a stone water cistern, tiled runnels, and a "wetland pond"—to the garden. Breezeways provide shaded passage for visitors but also add architectural interest and focal points; massive stone walls help absorb the Texas sun but harmoniously blend with the stone used in the walkways and the rock outcroppings in the gardens. Overhanging eaves shade windows and interiors from the intense sun while at the same time adding graceful lines to the roofs. All these are examples of beauty resulting from meeting functional needs with an ecological sensitivity that contributed to the LEED certification.

Using humble materials

The commitment to preserve and promote the use of native plants is the driving force of this organization, like the Crosby Arboretum. The mission of the Lady Bird Johnson Wildflower Center on a national level is to help each region appreciate, preserve, and protect what grows in its own backyard—its indigenous or humble plants.

Indigenous plants are the focus of their programs, but the use of indigenous or locally made materials in the buildings also adds to the humble and regionally

A water storage cistern greets visitors at the entrance to the Lady Bird Johnson Wildflower Center and with its prominence emphasizes the importance of water resources in the region.

A grain storage silo in the public garden draws from the agricultural heritage of the Texas Hill Country and celebrates vernacular forms of architecture. Instead of grain or corn, the silo stores native plant seeds now.

Limestone structures hearken back to the days when Germans settled the region; here a tiled gutter that captures and directs rainwater becomes an ornamental feature.

appropriate nature of the center. All the stone used at the center is native to the region or to Texas. The sandstone comes from near Lampasas, the limestone from Comfort, and the flagstone from Dryden. The tin roofs and siding are from local manufacturers; the exquisite broad floor planks of pine in the auditorium, the gift shop, and the visitors' gallery are recycled building material. In 2001 the historic Driskill-Scarbrough Carriage House from central Austin was moved to the site to be recycled as a multipurpose educational and gallery space.

The materials incorporated in the gardens become more rustic or naturalistic the farther away from the main buildings visitors venture. The flagstone-paved courtyards and walkways transition to sand or gravel pathways just beyond the central courtyard. Similarly, beyond the main buildings, lumber used to create overhangs transitions to knotty logs, weathered to a silvery gray, that form an overhead structure to partially shade a long walkway.

Marrying the inside to the outside

After passing through an archway near the entrance to the center, visitors come into a courtyard defined by various buildings surrounding it on three sides. This outdoor room functions like the hub of a wheel, connecting the visitors' gallery, the restroom building, the gift shop, and various other meeting rooms and offices. At the center of the outdoor room is a spring garden, a circular water feature providing a cooling feeling while replicating the natural springs of the Texas Hill Country.

Some of the rooms off the courtyard have windows in the outside walls, so that the savanna and clusters of oaks at the perimeter of the property are revealed in panoramic views and become the focus for visitors who have just stepped inside. Thus, some of the most dramatic and expansive vistas on the property are enjoyed from indoors.

Breezeways or covered walkways extend from the buildings out into the gardens; these provide some of the shade and shelter associated with the buildings. As visitors move to outdoor spaces, the transition from inside to outside is gradual and therefore more pleasant.

Various sitting pavilions—three-sided limestone alcoves—also bring some of the comforts associated with indoor spaces out into the garden. Visitors can sit on benches protected from drying winds and hot sun while fully immersed in looking at the garden and its plants.

Involving the visitor

Entering the center, visitors walk beside a raised stone aqueduct to a wall where water tumbles over what looks like the ruins of a foundation of a substantial stone building and then into a rectangular garden pool—another water storage cistern. Through the archway of the wall, visitors then pass into the courtyard garden

Rustic logs form a structure above a walkway. The structure connects the buildings to the garden while providing some shade from the hot Texas sun.

Walls mimicking the ruins of old houses serve to add structure to the gardens and bring the plantings and architecture together.

With windows shaded by overhanging eaves, buildings remain energy efficient while still providing expansive views, keeping the visitor connected to the outside while learning from exhibits inside.

Shelters made of local stone provide shade for those gazing at the garden, thereby bringing some of the comfort of the inside to the outside.

Rainwater captured from the roofs of buildings flows through this reproduced aqueduct to a cistern at the entrance of the center, stressing the prominent role water plays in shaping the sense of place in this region of Texas.

Captured rainwater stored in this pool allows aquatic plants of Texas to be exhibited. The movement and sound of the water guarantee an engaging sequence of experiences as visitors first enter the site.

The lookout tower provides a way for visitors to gain a broad overview of the gardens and the surrounding landscape.

The savannas surrounding the garden areas are managed to maintain the native grasses and wildflowers of the Texas prairie.

where water gurgles and wells up in a spring. Thus, within a few short minutes of entering the site, visitors quickly become engaged by the sight and sound of water in the garden. Thoughts of the outside world are replaced by thoughts and observations of the garden. After this dramatic entry sequence gains visitors' attention, they are then open to discovery of the gardens and natural areas. Engaged, they notice distinct styles, enjoy native plant palettes, and learn about the natural and cultural heritage of Texas.

Circular trails one quarter to one mile in length lead away from the central gardens, engaging visitors more fully in the site. The Woodland Trail features pecan, post, red and live oak, and elm—all species common to Hill Country woodlands. Walking the Restoration and Research Trail, visitors can learn how fire, grazing, and other land management practices affect Hill Country habitat. The Savanna Meadow Trail features the spring wildflowers that have become symbols of Texas—bluebonnets and Indian paintbrush (*Lupinus texensis* and *Castilleja indivisa*).

SUPERSTITION SPRINGS CENTER

I would guess there are thousands of shopping malls dotting cities across America, and like cookie-cutter subdivision houses, they reveal little to nothing about the part of the country they're in. If you were dropped into most malls, it would be hard to guess where you were. From the storefronts, to the two shopping tiers, to the open food courts, they all have a sameness to them, a fact that's been referred to as the homogenization of America. By contrast, the landscape of the hundred-acre Superstition Springs Center in Mesa, Arizona, designed by Christy Ten Eyck, exemplifies the principles outlined in this book. The shopping complex opened in 1990 and features nearly 150 stores, restaurants, or services and 6352 parking spaces. You may find the same books in the Borders there that you find in the Borders in your local mall, or the same fast food, but if you were dropped down in the parking lot, it wouldn't take you long to realize that you weren't in Kansas anymore.

Capturing the sense of place

Named after the mountain range that's visible from the parking lot, the center has a landscape design inspired by the Superstition Springs region. The pedestrian walkway that forms a spine through the parking lot resembles a desert walk among native plants since planting berms block the view of the cars and fine gravel is underfoot. This main entryway has more in common with a trail in an Arizona park than with an urban shopping experience. Palo verde, aloe, penstemon, and cactus interspersed among boulders create an entry experience comparable to walking the paths of the nearby Desert Botanical Garden.

The historically important activity of mining in the Superstition Mountains gave rise to the architectural elements added to the landscape. An outdoor water feature mimics the mining sluices that for the most part are now relics in the western landscape. Interpretive panels even document the story of the Lost Dutchman Mine—one of the most famous gold mining stories in Arizona.

An outdoor structure that serves as a rest stop and gathering space draws inspiration from the indigenous Indian ruins of Arizona. Its circular tower form, while clearly modern, hearkens back to ancient Indian ruins.

Walls made of patterned concrete block partially enclosing the play area make reference to both the famous Arizona Biltmore Hotel and Taliesin West, Frank Lloyd Wright's western home in Scottsdale, and his experimentation with eco-

This pedestrian walkway captures the sense of the region's natural areas so successfully that it's hard to believe it's set in the middle of the parking lot of a major shopping mall.

This modern tower that serves as a gathering space borrows from the architectural heritage of the region, taking inspiration for its form from Anasazi ruins.

The neutral colors of this precast concrete block wall blend with the colors of the desert and stone, while the material makes reference to work that Frank Lloyd Wright is known for in the Phoenix area.

This man-made canyon captures the feel of special natural areas in Arizona, thereby celebrating the spirit of the region's landscapes.

The playground expresses an appreciation of the flora and fauna of the Superstition Mountains, with regionally meaningful sculptures of desert reptiles.

nomical precast blocks, which he used for a period of his career. Thus, architectural influences prevalent in Arizona over a broad span of time are played back in this modern context.

The Canyon Walk, a path that descends into the play area, is true to its name. Realistic artificial boulders create the feel of walking through an Arizona canyon. Along the way all views to the cars and shopping complex are effectively blocked out, lending a sense of surprise and magic to arrival at the playground area.

The gold mining heritage of the Superstition Mountains is acknowledged in the design of this water feature that resembles a mining sluice. The fountain can be covered to become a stage in the center of the outdoor amphitheater.

The playground draws upon the creatures found living in the Superstition Mountains and the surrounding desert. Kids can climb on three giant lizards grouped together to form a "jungle gym"; they can slide down the back of a huge gila monster, another desert dweller.

Deriving beauty from function

Much like the Brandywine River Museum, the Superstition Springs Center parking lot is able to provide beauty while still functioning as an expansive parking lot. Walking from their cars to the entrance, traveling by way of the "botanical walk," shoppers can see desert wildflowers, native trees and shrubs in bloom, and cacti and succulents with striking architectural forms.

The water feature created by the abstraction of a mining sluice also serves as an amphitheater for outdoor performances. The pool is covered to become a stage, and terraced circular tiers around the water feature form seating areas. With the waterfall from the sluice animating the space, the area doesn't look empty or without a focal point when it's not in use as an amphitheater. (This area was renovated in 2005–2006, so it may function in a different way presently.)

Economical concrete block walls serve to contain distinct portions of the landscape.

The playground, with its sculptural pieces serving the purpose of giving children a place to play, is also a pleasure to walk through and to view. Without children, it's more like a wild sculptural park than a playground.

Using humble materials

The botanical walkway through the parking lot is simply gravel—a surprising use of a humble material in this setting. The concrete blocks forming gray walls with several patterns that separate the Canyon Walk and the play area are an economical building material; at the same time, the texture and color of the blocks blend with that of the boulders.

While changing displays of colorful annuals adorn some of the raised planter beds in the tiers of the amphitheater, even here, a classic Arizona native tree—a palo verde—is at the center of each. All the plants along the botanical walkway are natives, most salvaged from the site or other building sites in advance of development.

Marrying the inside to the outside

The outdoor amphitheater at this shopping complex provides a way to bring performance activities outside, which is again surprising, given the retail focus of the operations that take place inside. To help with the transition from the bright Arizona sun to the relative darkness of the interior of the shopping mall and vice versa, walkways with a metal trellis framework overhead extend from the doorways. The partial shade and partial sense of enclosure these offer makes the transition from inside to outside less abrupt and therefore more pleasurable.

Inside, the shopping complex features beds planted with cactus and succulents, although at the time of my last visit, they were struggling in the low-light environment. The goal in using these plants was clearly to bring the sense of the outdoors inside, to integrate the indoor spaces with the exterior landscapes, although it would no doubt be easier to fill the beds with common tropical houseplants. The interior spaces also feature natural colors, stone, and wood, thereby carrying some qualities of the outdoors inside.

Involving the visitor

Before shoppers get involved with shopping and bargain hunting inside, they're provided with opportunities to become engaged in the landscape as they travel the botanical walkway with its rich and varied composition of native plants. If they venture through the Canyon Walk, they can also experience narrow canyon walls and watch their kids play on the playground's sculptural forms.

In the amphitheater, the mesmerizing sight of water cascading off the end of the high sluice and the sound of this cascading water provide refreshment. With wind, shoppers might even feel a little water mist on their faces, cooling them and connecting them to the landscape before they carry on with their shopping.

In this chapter, we've looked at a handful of gardens—ranging in size, geographical location, and function—that embrace the five principles. Studying stellar examples such as these can help you imagine how you might apply the principles in creating your own garden space or landscape. I hope what you've learned here will inspire you to create, preserve, and cherish spaces that honor their place, their time, and the needs of those frequenting them in genuine and engaging ways.

REFERENCES

Aichele, K. Porter. 1977. Essay in *The Wharton Esherick Museum Studio and Collection*. Paoli, Pennsylvania: Wharton Esherick Museum.

Bye, A. E. 1983. *Art into Landscape, Landscape into Art*. Mesa, Arizona: PDA Publishers.

Carey, Art. 2005. Luxe logs. *Philadelphia Inquirer*, March 18, 2005.

Cronon, William. 2003. *Changes in the Land: Indians, Colonists, and the Ecology of New England*. 20th anniversary ed. New York: Hill and Wang, 1983.

England, Yvonne. 1995. Bring on the bubbly: Enliven the garden with an easy-to-build millstone fountain. *Fine Gardening* (August): 46–47.

Frederick, William H., Jr. 1975. *100 Great Garden Plants*. Reprint. Portland, Oregon: Timber Press, 1986.

———. 1992. *The Exuberant Garden and the Controlling Hand: Plant Combinations for American Gardens*. Boston: Little, Brown.

Giovannini, Joseph. 1987. Our land of fences. *New York Times*, August 13, 1987.

Hymans, Edward. 1971. *A History of Gardens and Gardening*. New York: Praeger.

Ivy, Robert Adams, Jr. 1992. *Fay Jones*. Washington, D.C.: American Institute of Architects Press.

Jekyll, Gertrude. 1901. *Home and Garden*. New York: Longmans, Green & Co.

Jensen, Jens. 1939. *Siftings*. Reprint. Baltimore, Maryland: Johns Hopkins University Press, 1990.

Karson, Robin. 1989. *Fletcher Steele, Landscape Architect—An Account of the Garden Maker's Life, 1885–1971*. New York: Abrams.

Koren, Leonard. 1994. *Wabi-Sabi for Artists, Designers, Poets and Philosophers*. Berkeley, California: Stone Bridge Press.

Kuck, Loraine. 1968. *The World of the Japanese Garden: From Chinese to Modern Landscape Art*. New York and Tokyo: John Wetherhill.

Kuo, Frances, and William Sullivan. 2001. Environment and crime in the inner city: Does vegetation reduce crime? *Environment and Behavior* 33(3): 343–367.

Lawrence, Robyn Griggs. 2004. *The Wabi-Sabi House: The Japanese Art of Imperfect Beauty*. New York: Clarkson Potter.

Leopold, Aldo. 1949. *A Sand County Almanac*. Special commemorative edition. New York: Oxford University Press, 1987.

Lewis, Charles A. 1996. *Green Nature / Human Nature: The Meaning of Plants in Our Lives*. Urbana and Chicago, Illinois: University of Illinois Press.

Linden-Ward, Blanche. 1987. Stan Hywet. *Landscape Architecture* (July/August): 66–70.

Madson, John. 1982. *Where the Sky Began: Land of the Tallgrass Prairie*. San Francisco: Sierra Club Books.

McHarg, Ian L. 1969. *Design with Nature*. Garden City, New York: Doubleday.

Michener, James A. 1968. *Iberia*. Reissue edition. New York: Fawcett, 1984.

Mitchell, Henry. 1981. *The Essential Earthman: Henry Mitchell on Gardening*. Reprint. Bloomington, Indiana: Indiana University Press, 2003.

Ockenga, Starr. 1998. *Earth on Her Hands: The American Woman in Her Garden*. New York: Clarkson Potter.

Roberts, Edith A., and Elsa Rehmann. 1929. *American Plants for American Gardens*. Reprint. Athens, Georgia: University of Georgia Press, 1996.

Smithers, Peter. 1995. *Adventures of a Gardener*. London: The Harvill Press with the Royal Horticultural Society.

Takei, Jiro, and Marc P. Keane. 2001. *Sakuteiki: Vision of the Japanese Garden. A Modern Translation of Japan's Gardening Classic*. Tokyo: Tuttle.

Verey, Rosemary, and Ellen Samuels. 1984. *The American Woman's Garden*. Boston: Little, Brown.

Wharton, Edith. 1904. *Italian Villas and Their Gardens*. New York: Century Company.

Wilkinson, Norman B. 1972. *E. I. du Pont Botaniste: The Beginning of a Tradition.* Charlottesville: University Press of Virginia.

Wright, Frank Lloyd. 1954. *The Natural House.* New York: Bramhall House.

Wright, Mary, and Russel Wright. 1950. *Guide to Easier Living.* Reprint. Layton, Utah: Gibbs Smith, 2003.

Wright, Russel. 1970. *A Garden of Woodland Paths.* Garrison, New York: J. M. Kaplan Fund.

INDEX

Page numbers in *italic* indicate illustrations.